THE
ISAIAH 13
INVASION OF
AMERICA

UNFOLDING PROPHECY
AT THE SOUTHERN BORDER

DAVID BRENNAN, SR.

The Isaiah 13 Invasion of America

Website for this book: www.SwordofDavid.com
Published by Teknon Publishing, Covington, Louisiana

ISBN: 978-1-7324135-4-2
Retailers and distributors qualify for special discounts on bulk purchases. For more information, email Teknon Publishing at:
SwordofDavid@Yahoo.com

CONTENTS

Confession of Faith

Jesus Christ of Nazareth, placed in the womb of woman by the Spirit of God, crucified on a Roman cross nearly two thousand years ago, died, rose from the dead, and is the resurrection and the eternal life of those placing their trust and faith in Him alone. He is the <u>only</u> way to salvation, by faith and trust in Him alone for the cleansing of sins. No person can save themselves.

He is the Son of the living God, true God and true man, whom the Father sent into the world on a mission of salvation for mankind, overcoming the forces of darkness through His light, guiding believers by the presence of the Holy Spirit, and working His holy will not by might nor by power, but by His Spirit.

The Bible is the unerring Word of God, given to mankind for salvation and guidance, written through the hand of the prophets guided by the Holy Spirit, the source of truth in a world filled with deception.

All prophetic utterances in the Bible will come to pass in due time.

1

INVASION AT THE SOUTHERN BORDER

When Americans express concern about events at the southern border, it is typically framed in political terms. And this is understandable. From a political standpoint, the flood of illegal entries across the border is both dangerous and politically destabilizing. But it is also something else. It is unnatural. What is meant by that is that since the founding of the nation, there has never been anything like it. Yes, there has always been cross border movement from South and Central America. But what has been taking place is so far off the scale of all previous movements as to be unnatural. Especially what has been happening since Mr. Joseph Biden took power.

America has always been the land of the immigrant. Because native Indians are the only true indigenous people. Everyone else and their ancestors either willingly or unwillingly arrived on these shores according to what page of American history is looked at. But never has it been the policy of a major political party to encourage a mass migration of Third World people into the country. Until now.

Such a policy is inherently destructive, lowering the wages of the most vulnerable American workers, bringing diseases into the country that had long been eradicated, and allowing massive voter fraud with large numbers of non-citizens voting. And they obviously vote for the party whose allies and workers encouraged them to make the long trip into the promised land of welfare debit cards, free phones, free medical care, and free education. With such a lure thrown into the heart of the Third World, who can resist?

In exchange for all these freely given benefits, America has received legions of individuals who have no love for America or the American people. As a result, political polling indicates illegal immigration has become the number one concern for a majority of voters.

Yet, despite raising the ire of people across party lines, somehow no strong action is taken to shut down the border. In fact, Mr. Biden has chosen to stop all efforts to do so. And not only has this phenomenon of working against the will of the people been unfolding in the United States, but across Western Europe as well. It could be summed up as taking place in the West in general. All of which indicates that an agenda of massive proportions has been unfolding against the Western block of nations. It also indicates on a broader scale that some world entity has gained control over a number of nations, including the United States. An entity whose policy is the execution of soft invasions of all nations under their control.

The Isaiah 13 Invasion of America presents the case that this mass invasion at the southern border of the United States and across Western Europe was prophetically foretold to take place. That it is fulfilling a very specific prophecy given by the prophet Isaiah. As will be shown, all the elements of this prophecy are now unfolding with uncanny accuracy. Yet, despite this, the church appears oblivious to the prophetic significance of the unfolding drama at the southern border. A drama that is one of the grandest signs of the approach of the end times. Without the invasion of nations by those "from a far country," which has unfolded in the West, the end times cannot take place. It is a critical piece of the end time puzzle.

Perhaps its significance has been missed because it is viewed as a political problem. And this is understandable because it is political. But it is also a prophecy. And the likely reason the church is unaware of its unfolding is that it has been difficult to take this prophecy literally because no nation has ever allowed itself to suffer the dangers of a mass invasion. Millions of people entering countries of whom they know nothing. As a result, the literal fulfillment of the prophecy seemed very unlikely. Until now.

Isaiah's prophecy has likely faced the same hurdle that the prophecies foretelling the literal return of Israel faced. Before 1948, who could reasonably think such a thing was meant to be taken literally? However, in that year the Jews did return as a nation in the land of their fathers after being dispersed for almost two-thousand years. Although the literal words of various prophets said they would return, it was a prophecy that appeared impossible to ever literally fulfill. Thus, over the ages, students of Bible prophecy did not take it literally.

Yet, after it happened in 1948, a multitude of Bible prophecy students realized the prophetic words were meant to be taken literally. And it is likely this is the case with the words of Isaiah. Who would ever believe a nation would allow itself to suffer a mass invasion? It appears so unlikely that other interpretations of Isaiah's words have been embraced. But with the literal unfolding of this prophecy, that should now change.

Not only did Isaiah detail that a mass invasion would take place with masses of foreigners entering nations, many having ill will in their hearts, but ominously he also informs us what the result of the invasion will be. And since the first part of the prophecy has taken place, then we should believe the second part will also fulfill exactly as it is given. Effectively, it is an army of the Antichrist that is building up within nations he could not otherwise directly invade. It is an army that is destined to bring great destruction to America and Western Europe.

The prophet also tells of the response of citizens within the attacked nations against those who came in to do them great harm. And it is that response by those attacked where the prophet Daniel also comes into the picture. It is his words that appear to tell of the result of the war within America's borders that is coming. The words of both Isaiah and Daniel paint an important mosaic of end time Bible prophecy as it relates to America.

The extreme nature of the invasion has created political divisions within the nation like never before. But as more and more Americans of all political persuasions hear of the masses of third-world people coming in, there appears to be a nonpartisan agreement among the American people against it. But, ironically, not with the political leaders. The leadership of the Democratic Party appears absolute in its desire to see the invasion continue. Even as danger for the nation grows.

For example, in December 2023, over 300,000 illegal immigrants were apprehended attempting to cross the southern border—the highest number ever recorded for a single month and a staggering increase from December 2020 during President Donald Trump's tenure. Since President Joe Biden took office, until 2024, more than 10 million illegal border entries have occurred, highlighting a growing and urgent national security threat. Again, it seems to have been the policy of Mr. Biden to allow as many as possible within the nation. But, of course, is it his policy or someone else? A fair question with the revelation of Mr. Biden's mental impairment indicating he has been someone's puppet all along.

But it is not just Mr. Biden. It is true that he has dismantled Trump's border policies that were proving effective. However, Mr. Biden's administration has had the help of Senate Democrats in blocking stringent border legislation. So severe has been the refusal of Biden administration officials and allies to address the issue that House Republicans have aggressively gone after one of the main culprits behind the policy of allowing the invasion.

In January 2024, the House Homeland Security Committee advanced articles of impeachment against Mr. Biden's Homeland Security Secretary Alejandro Mayorkas, a central figure in this crisis. After an investigation of Mr. Mayorkas and his department, it was concluded there was extensive evidence of his disregard for laws, court orders, and rulings. He has been accused of betraying the trust of Congress and the American people, even lying under oath about the border's security. Going after him represented the first time in over a century that a cabinet member was impeached.

The threat of terrorism from the invasion is also real and growing. Since Mr. Biden's inauguration, a multitude of suspected terrorists have attempted to enter the U.S. In January 2023, the House passed critical legislation to ban members of Hamas and other terror groups involved in attacks against Israel from entering the U.S. Something never thought to be needed but for the openness of the border. Many people point out that "a nation without borders is not a nation," causing governors to begin acting. In response to the open border in Texas, Governor Greg Abbott challenged the Biden administration on the basis that the U.S. Constitution grants states the authority to defend their citizens.

The constitutional definition of an invader involves two key elements: entering sovereign territory and bearing enmity towards the sovereign. An immigrant without enmity isn't an invader, nor is an enemy who remains outside our borders.

The crisis is also fueled by Mexico's powerholders, driven by money and leverage over the U.S. The Mexican state and cartels are intertwined, with President Andrés Manuel López Obrador (AMLO) openly siding with the Sinaloa cartel. There is a lot of money from the drug trade through an open border. And that money has made its way into politics. As a result, he vows military protection for cartels against the U.S.

In place of the federal government acting, the state of Texas has taken some steps to protect its citizens. Such as...

- Transporting migrants to liberal localities nationwide to highlight the border crisis.
- Utilizing its military forces, including the Texas Army National Guard, in Operation Lone Star.
- Constructing effective border barriers, including buoy barriers in the Rio Grande.
- Enacting laws that allow Texas law enforcement to intercept and effectively deport illegal entrants.

Although the federal government should be implementing these measures, fulfilling the most basic constitutional responsibility, it has taken Texas to defend its citizens. Governor Abbott asserts that Texas is upholding both state and U.S. constitutional law, wherein Article I, Section 10, mandates state self-defense against invasion.

And all of this raises the serious question of why, for the first time in U.S. history, an American government has refused to protect the American people. More on that later.

Since the federal government has refused to address the invasion, the Republican led House of Representatives has introduced legislation declaring the crisis at the southern border an invasion with the aim to strengthen states' legal standing in federal court, so they have the right to defend their citizens. Again, raising the question as to why this is even necessary.

For nearly 250 years, America has been a government of, by, and for the people. Yet today, our nation faces a grave security threat at our southern border, exacerbated by a federal government that enables the violation of federal laws. A nation without borders ceases to be a nation. A government that neglects its duty to secure its people is not just negligent but inhumane.

In response to Texas beginning to take action, Democratic politicians began pushing to federalize the Texas National Guard. A move would mark the first time in history that a president activates American armed forces to make its citizens less safe. Demonstrating the depth of commitment to open borders by the Democratic Party. Although 25 Republican governors have asserted states' rights to self-defense, citing an estimated ten million illegal entries in the past three years, no Democrat governor has joined them despite their states also being overrun.

CONCLUSION

Before getting to the prophecies of Isaiah and Daniel, it is important to understand that the threat to America is vastly more serious than described in this chapter. This chapter simply paints a broad picture of what is happening politically relative to the border and its general impact. But nowhere was it intended to address the entry into the United States of a literal enemy military force. The best place to develop that picture is to start with the words of ten former FBI department heads.

2

THE FBI LETTER: THE FOREIGN ARMY GATHERING WITHIN AMERICA

The last time America fought a foreign army on its soil was during the War of 1812. That war took place only 29 years after the thirteen fledgling colonies defeated the massive British army. And once again, 1812 pitted the United States against the British army. It would eventually end with the Treaty of Ghent in 1814 and would be the last time the British Empire would attempt to fight the newly formed American nation.

With strong growth in its population and economy, the nation founded by Washington would become too strong for any European colonial power to intimidate again. Instead, over time it would become the real power in the western hemisphere. As such, America issued a warning to the world in the form of the Monroe Doctrine.

Regarded as a guaranteed military response to any European incursion into the hemisphere.

As a result, many wise observers of the American experience have noted the virtual impossibility for America to be invaded from outside. Others have added that the only way the nation could be taken down would be from within. And such an observation has always carried with it overtures of a conspiracy.

During the rise of Hitler there was real concern that the Nazi regime, after conquering all of Europe, would turn its attention to South America and eventually the United States. But with the tide of war eventually turning against the madman, the threat of invasion and war on American soil faded.

Those who said America could never be successfully invaded from the outside were right. It appears that she can't be. Unfortunately, those who said the only way America can be harmed is from within appear to also be right. The culmination of America being successfully assaulted from within has now happened. With a massive and growing foreign army within the United States awaiting the order to attack.

THE FBI

Sometimes it takes an individual from a sensitive government position to retire before they can speak freely. So, it appears to be the case with ten former FBI agents, most of whom were leaders in some of the most sensitive positions relating to threats against America. It's not just these agents who are sounding the alarm. But the director of the FBI.

The Director of the FBI, Mr. Wray, has been before Congress on multiple occasions, warning about the growing dangers to the nation from the open border. But it is a letter from ten retired FBI agents, that strikes a chord of concern in line with the threat level. What they have to say is not for the faint hearted. But it is necessary to understand in order to appreciate that what is happening at the southern border is unfolding according to the ancient warning of the prophet Isaiah.

To more fully appreciate the weight of what you are about to read, consider the credentials of the ten agents and what positions they held before retiring. Here is the list taken directly from their letter:

Mr. Kevin R. Brock
Assistant Director, Directorate of Intelligence
Federal Bureau of Investigation (Ret.)
Principal Deputy Director
National Counterterrorism Center (Former)

Mr. Chris Swecker
Assistant Director, Criminal Investigative Division
Federal Bureau of Investigation (Ret.)

Mr. Timothy J. Healy
Director, Terrorist Screening Center
Federal Bureau of Investigation (Ret.)

Mr. Ruben Garcia, Jr.
Executive Assistant Director, Criminal, Cyber, Response and Service Branch
Federal Bureau of Investigation

Mr. Mark Morgan
Assistant Director, Training Division
Federal Bureau of Investigation (Ret.)
Acting Commissioner, Customs and Border Protection (Former)
Chief, U.S. Border Patrol (Former)

Mr. David Szady
Assistant Director, Counterintelligence Division
Federal Bureau of Investigation (Ret.)

Mr. Jody Weis
Special Agent in Charge, Philadelphia
Federal Bureau of Investigation (Ret.)
Superintendent, Chicago Police Department (Former)

Mr. David Mitchell
Special Agent in Charge, Milwaukee
Federal Bureau of Investigation (Ret.)
Commissioner of Safety, Tennessee
Director of Homeland Security, Tennessee (Former)

Mr. William Gavin
Assistant Director, Inspection Division
Federal Bureau of Investigation (Ret.)

Mr. Timothy McNally
Assistant Director, Los Angeles Division
Federal Bureau of Investigation (Ret.)

As is obvious from a quick perusal of the positions held by those who wrote the letter you are about to read, they are substantial individuals. And it is apparent that it is because they are retired that they can write this letter to top members of congress without fear of political retribution. And, no doubt, although retired, they continue to have contact with their active FBI friends and associates. What you are about to read indicates a gathering of a great army from enemy nations within the United States. The first in its history and setting the stage for the fulfillment of Isaiah 13.

THE FBI LETTER

January 17, 2024

The Honorable Mike Johnson
Speaker of the House
H-232 The Capitol
Washington, DC 20515-0001

The Honorable Charles Schumer
Majority Leader
322 Hart Senate Office Building
Washington, DC 20510

The Honorable Mike Turner
Chair, House Permanent Select Committee
on Intelligence
2183 Rayburn HB
Washington, DC 20515

The Honorable Mark Warner
Chair, Senate Select Committee on Intelligence

703 Hart Senate Building
Washington, DC 20510

The Honorable Mark Green
Chair, Committee on Homeland Security
2446 Rayburn HOB
Washington, DC 20515

The Honorable Gary Peters
Chair, Senate Committee on Homeland Security
and Government Affairs
724 Hart Senate Office Building
Washington, DC 20510

Subject: The United States is Facing a New and
Imminent Danger

Dear Mr. Speaker, Senate Majority Leader, Chairmen,

As former senior executives of the Federal Bureau
of Investigation with deep experience combating
dangers to the nation, we write to express our concern about a current, specific threat that may be one
of the most pernicious ever to menace the United
States.

The danger arises from the nature of the threat
itself. Wars and espionage and bombings and riots
are sadly familiar delivery systems of instability,
intimidation, and insecurity. The country has faced
these and more throughout its history and has held
together, though not without struggle.

The threat we call out today is new and unfamiliar. In its modern history the U.S. has never suffered an invasion of the homeland and, yet, one is unfolding now. Military aged men from across the globe, many from countries or regions not friendly to the United States, are landing in waves on out soil by the thousands – not by splashing ashore from a ship or parachuting from a plane but rather by foot across a border that has been accurately advertised around the world as largely unprotected with ready access granted.

It would be difficult to overstate the danger represented by the presence inside our borders of what is comparatively a multi-division army of young single adult males from hostile nations and regions whose background, intent, or allegiance is completely unknown. They include individuals encountered by border officials and then possibly released into the country, along with a shockingly high estimate of "gotaways- meaning those who have entered and evaded apprehension.

In light of such a daunting, unprecedented penetration by uninvited foreign actors, it is reasonable to assert that the country possesses dramatically diminished national security at this time. The nation's military and laws and other natural protective barriers that have provided traditional security in the past have been thoroughly circumvented over the past three years.

In 2021, the demographics of those crossing the porous southern boundary started to shift. Young men from around the world traveling alone and holding questionable motivations dramatically increased in number to become the most common profile of those breaching the nation's borders. A startling number have been found on the terrorist watchlist or are from countries designated as State Sponsors of Terror distinctly unfriendly to the United States.

This is particularly alarming in light of the Hamas terror attack on Israel last October 7. Those of us who have fought terrorism know that, historically, successful terrorist attacks invite mimicry. We know, as well, that terror leaders intentionally cultivate throngs of young men possessing a certain easily manipulated personality type to carry out atrocities.

It is stark to say so, but having a large number of young males now within our borders who could begin attacking gatherings of unarmed citizens, in imitation of 10/7 and at the behest of a foreign terror group, must be considered a distinct possibility. We would be remiss not to call out this potentially grave threat in the most direct terms. The warning lights are blinking.

And yet, this very real concern does not seem to be getting the focus it logically deserves. The Director of the FBI has correctly assessed an elevated threat level since 10/7. But relatively little discussion has followed highlighting unsecured borders as a significant cause of this increasingly dangerous environment. It is a troubling concern that needs illumination, not avoidance.

Any violation of the nation's immigration laws increases risks, but the surge in numbers of single, military aged males descending upon American cities and towns is alarming and perilous. Additionally, they are not just from terror linked regions, but from China and Russia as well- hostile adversaries of the U.S. with aspirations to devastate national infrastructure.

For these reasons, elements of this recent surge are likely no accident or coincidence. These men are potential operators in what appears to be an accelerated and strategic penetration, a soft invasion, designed to gain internal access to a country that cannot be invaded militarily in order to inflict catastrophic damage if and when the enemies deem it necessary.

The new reality, this "never seen before" threat deserves greater attention. The borders need to be secured against these young men and those already here illegally must be identified and removed without delay. This will take the coordinated, cooperative efforts of the FBI, Department of Homeland Security and the rest of the Intelligence Community to achieve.

We encourage these actions and much greater Congressional attention to this threat. The country has been invaded, an invasion that will continue as long as the nation's enemies perceive it will be tolerated. Until it is stopped, the United States is extraordinarily less safe and secure. Knowing all of this, it would be a shameful travesty if some terrible attack, a preventable attack, were to occur against innocent Americans or the infrastructure that keeps the nation safe and functioning.

The government will have failed grievously in its duty to protect.

Sincerely,
(SIGNED BY THOSE INITIALLY MENTIONED)

According to the letter, the current, specific threat is "one of the most pernicious ever to menace the United States." Pointing out that "in its modern history the U.S. has never suffered an invasion of the homeland and, yet one is unfolding now." The last invasion of America dates to 1812. Yet, because of the open southern border, "Military aged men from across the globe, many from countries or regions not friendly to the United States, are landing in waves on our soil by the thousands."

All the critical advantages of a strong military, strict immigration laws, and natural barriers that have provided protection for America to grow peaceable and prosper have been circumvented. And they conclude that, "the country possesses dramatically diminished national security at this time." Because America is a large country, it would take a large army operating within civilian areas to bring the level of destruction that would bring the nation to a standstill. It would also result in a horrifying death toll as unarmed civilians scramble to find safety. In the letter, they address how large they believe the army has grown.

The estimate they give is that there is "the presence inside our borders of what is comparatively a multi-division army of young single adult males from hostile nations and regions whose background, intent, or allegiance is completely unknown." Within the armed forces of a nation, a single division typically consists of approximately 20,000 men. There is a multi-division army already present within the United States! But what is their goal?

The FBI agents provide their scenario of what kind of attacks should be expected because "the surge in numbers of single, military aged males descending upon American cities and towns is alarming and perilous." The enemy army could "begin attacking gatherings of unarmed citizens." And certainly, they will seek to "devastate national infrastructure." They go on to point out that the surge in military-age single males is no accident but "an accelerated and strategic penetration, a soft invasion, designed to gain internal access to a country that cannot be invaded militarily in order to inflict catastrophic damage if and when the enemies deem it necessary."

What Others are Saying

Gordon Chang, an accomplished author who lived in China for two decades and is considered an expert on their goals and strategic vision, has deep national security credentials, having advised the National Intelligence Council, the Central Intelligence Agency, the US State Department, and the US Department of Defense on Communist China. This is what he had to say during a TV network interview concerning the open southern border relative to the Chinese threat to the United States.

"Across that border we are seeing Chinese soldiers come across. And really what we are talking about is China putting together the infrastructure in the US to attack the US. Clearly, we've got to secure that border or we're going to be fighting on our own soil."[1]

Chang is not alone. Real journalists not hampered by political restraints have investigated what is happening in Central America relative to the southern border. One of the best is a 24-year veteran former Customs official and number two in command of the Arizona border control station, Mr. J.J. Carrell. In his book, *Invaded… The Intentional Destruction of the American Immigration System*, he details from a firsthand perspective what happened after Mr. Biden took power in January 2021.[2]

Before Mr. Biden, the border patrol arrested about 500 people a day across the entire 2000-mile border, and ICE would deport all of them. But after Mr. Biden took power, orders came down daily from Washington, D.C., to release all those arrested. The way it was handled was they were to begin releasing those arrested to United Nations non-government organizations (NGO's), who then in turn released them into America.[3]

Carrell goes on to say that on day one of Mr. Biden taking power, he issued 94 executive orders relating to the border that started the process of opening it. Indicating that an open border was a major (if not the major) policy goal of his administration. Actually, the goal of whoever was directing his administration. By the end of the first year, Mr. Biden issued 296 executive orders on the border, according to Carrell. All of which served to streamline entry and distribution into the United States.[4]

He indicated that in Mr. Biden's first year, the NOG's appeared clumsy in the operation of processing those illegally entering. However, by 2023, the process was operating with military efficiency. Literally, processing people within minutes of arriving with many wearing "Thank You Biden" shirts.

According to Carrell, the changes he saw made it clear that the entire effort was a major operation designed with the singular goal of facilitating the movement of persons illegally into the United States. And that there had to be many planning meetings of those involved in the effort. Carrell describes it as treason. And since many coming in appear to be part of a foreign military, their treason is historical.[5]

Underscoring the understanding on the part of those in the know concerning the growing threat, in May of 2024, the Associated Press reported President Trump had this to say concerning the large influx of Chinese single males coming through the southern border since Mr. Biden took power.

"They're coming in from China — 31, 32,000 over the last few months — and they're all military age, and they mostly are men," Trump said during a campaign rally last month in Schnecksville, Pennsylvania. "And it sounds like to me, are they trying to build a little army in our country? Is that what they're trying to do?"[6]

Near the end of his term, Mr. Trump signed an executive order banning investment by Americans in Chinese military companies posing as aerospace operations. But one of the first things Mr. Biden did after taking power was to reverse that order. Reopening American investment that effectively helped modernize the Chinese war machine.[7]

Another security element that grants China leverage over the U.S. is 5G communications. Although it has the potential to allow China access to communications throughout the US, Mr. Biden has given them an open door of distribution. But Chinese infiltration into the security complex of the US goes deeper.[8]

According to Lt. Col. Robert Maginnis, retired, "the Chinese have infiltrated the US probably as deeply as possible." Primarily operating out of Washington, D.C., and San Francisco, their spies have had in depth access to US political leaders who have access to sensitive national security information. One such instance is the case of California US Senator Diane Feinstein when it came out that her driver of 20 years was a Chinese spy. Another is the case of California US Representative Eric Swalwell. As a member of the highly sensitive intelligence committee, Swalwell had access to some of the most sensitive national security secrets. But apparently so did the Chinese spy he was sleeping with.[9]

These examples of Chinese infiltration into America only scratch the surface. Having access to the most sensitive national security information is perhaps why they have decided to send an invasion force across the southern border. An internal force is in place, ready to attack key infrastructure targets upon command while avoiding a direct military confrontation with the United States. Embracing the wisdom of Sun Tzu, ancient author of *The Art of War* who said:

"Avoid what is strong and strike at what is weak."

3

PROBING AMERICA'S DEFENSES

When an army gathers to attack, one of the first actions it engages in is to probe enemy defenses. Such probes are to learn how secure enemy defenses are, including the security of their communication system. Probing actions against the enemy reveals their reaction time as well as any weaknesses. Already this multi-divisional foreign army of young, single military-age males has begun probing America's defenses.

Since the war of 1812, no U.S. military base on American soil has been attacked. Obviously, the reason this has not happened for so long is because there has been no foreign army operating within the United States since that time. But with the open southern border, that has all changed.

On February 22, 2021, one month after Mr. Biden took power, reports of attempted breaches at military bases in the U.S. began coming in. According to Air & Space Forces Magazine, at the start of 2021, there were 13 attempted and successful beaches at Air National Guard bases in the U.S.[1] And the new trend would continue to increase.

The Wall Street Journal in September 2023 reported that "Chinese nationals, sometimes posing as tourists accessed military bases and other sensitive sites in the U.S. as many as 100 times in recent years. According to U.S. officials who describe the incidents as a potential espionage threat."[2]

According to the Epoch Times, in the first seven months of 2023, border agents have apprehended 48,500 Chinese illegal immigrants. In all of 2022, it was 52,700.[3] It should be noted that China is a closed country. Meaning that its citizens are not free to come and go as they please. Making it clear that those illegally entering through the southern border are being sent by the Chinese Communist government. It should also be noted that before Mr. Biden took power, the number of illegals from China was almost nonexistent.

The X-factor, if you will, is Mr. Biden. It was at the start of his term that the makeup of those illegally coming across the southern border radically changed to those from hostile regions and countries. Not before. His taking power in the United States appears to have been a green light for the enemies of America to send their forces flooding across the nation's border. Of these Chinese forces entering, Representative Pat Fallon of Texas says, "Dozens of incidents have come to light of Chinese nationals snapping photos near military installations and critical infrastructure such as reservoirs, claiming to be tourists—even when the facilities are rural and isolated."[4]

Admiral Daryl Caudle, commander of the U.S. Fleet Forces Command, concerning military base breaches in the U.S., reports,

"It's happening more and more. This is something we see probably two or three times a week where we're stopping these folks at the gate, and this is just Navy alone." But the Navy is certainly not alone among the branches of the military experiencing this new threat to the homeland.

According to Col. Philip Laing, chief of staff at Camp Pendleton Marine Corps Base in California, "the homeland is no longer a sanctuary"[5] of safety for the American people. A statement that has not been able to be spoken for a very long time in the land of the free. But a reflection of the drastic change in national security since individuals with conflicted loyalties took power.

At another Marine Corps base in Quantico, Virginia, two Jordanian illegal aliens attempted a breach in May 2024. Their effort was done by using a sophisticated identity. They claimed to both be Amazon delivery drivers. They had what looked like Amazon uniforms and truck decals representing the company as well. When they could not provide proper identification, they were asked to redirect their trucks for further inspection. The men then attempted to force their way forward until guards stopped their trucks.[6] Clearly, they were on a mission to probe the base without regard to their own personal safety.

As those efforts made weekly by illegal aliens to breach U.S. military bases across the country take place, FBI Director Christopher Wray has acknowledged the heightened risk to national security. Saying," I've never seen a time where all the threats or so many of the threats are all elevated, all exactly at the same time."[7] Yet despite this, it was the steadfast policy of the Biden Administration to fight all efforts to shut down illegal border entries. Considering the revelations of Mr. Biden's mental capabilities and that no person in that condition can fulfil the duties of President of the United States, the question is who has been pulling the strings in the background? That is a question that will be addressed later.

As part the effort to resist closing the border, the Biden Administration in October 2023 refused a Freedom of Information Act request by major media outlets to provide information on the nationalities of suspects on the terrorist watchlist who were released into the country. In the first three years after Mr. Biden took power, 360 individuals on the FBI's terrorist watchlist were apprehended. But since most crossing the open border are never apprehended, the real number is multiples of the 360. This compares to only 14 such apprehensions in the prior four years. But that threat, as serious as it is, pales in comparison to Special Interest Aliens (SIAs) that have crossed into the country.[8]

SIA's are individuals who are believed to potentially pose a threat to national security. Between October 2021 and October 2023, 70,000 such people entered the United States. And the pace of SIA's entering has dramatically increased as the U.S. presidential election approached with up to 50,000 in 2024 through May.[9] Again, these are the ones that can be counted. The real number is likely much higher.

The point of providing this information is to paint an accurate picture as to the magnitude of the threat now facing America. A threat that is no longer a potential one but one that is now in place. The imposition of which has been the literal policy of the Biden Administration. An administration that has been filled with appointees who previously worked for Mr. George Soros or an organization he controls.

What is clear is that the size of the foreign army that is amassing within the borders of America is enormous. Probably numbering in the hundreds of thousands. And their probes of military bases are an ominous sign. Which indicates that when they receive the order to attack, the first target will be U.S. military bases. And the reason is clear. They want access to the military hardware stored at the bases. If successful, what is presently a large but lightly armed foreign military now on American soil will become a large heavily armed one. It should be noted that local police forces are not capable of dealing with military hardware. Which also means that the loss of American lives will be catastrophic.

When the order to attack comes, the American public will be a major target to divert police assets from other targets. Unarmed civilians are an easy target to inflect gigantic casualties and sew confusion. But as easy as civilian gathering places are to target, it is the nation's infrastructure that this army will score its greatest victories. By knocking out the power grid as well as communications, America will be paralyzed. Yet those in the Biden Administration seek to block all attempts to stop the flow of additional enemy troops into the nation. And this raises the specter of treason at the highest levels of the U.S. government.

To attack U.S. military bases, the foreign army initially needs bases of its own. According to the Epoch Times in their July 24-30, 2024 edition, this is exactly what is happening. The article titled, "US Increases Scrutiny of Chinese Land Buys Near Military Bases," quoting Congressman Pat Fallon (R-Texas), those land purchases near military instillations are a "grave threat" to national security. According to Fallon, "I'm choosing my words carefully. I don't want to understate the threat because you can't overstate it."[10]

There is also the need for this foreign army to have funding. In July 2024, two Chinese nationals who entered the U.S. illegally were discovered to have $250,000 worth of gold bars in their possession. However, the Chinese government will not allow their citizens to depart the country with gold. Indicating the strong likelihood that the Chinese government sent them.[11] Considering the odds of catching those Chinese possessing that amount of gold, it is very likely that the number entering the country with large amounts of gold is vastly greater.

As bad as all of this sounds, there is a Biblical prophetic reason major leaders in America are allowing it to take place.

4

A TIME OF TRAITORS

In 2 Timothy 3, the church finds a lengthy description of the nature of men in the last days. Consider the first four verses, paying close attention to each unfortunate characteristic provided.

> ¹But know this, that in the last days perilous times will come: ² For men will be lovers of themselves, lovers of money, boasters, proud, blasphemers, disobedient to parents, unthankful, unholy, ³ unloving, unforgiving, slanderers, without self-control, brutal, despisers of good, ⁴ traitors, headstrong, haughty, lovers of pleasure rather than lovers of God,

The cabal that brought the world COVID-19, locking down the entire world, is the same one who introduced a rushed "vaccine" that has dramatically increased the mortality rate of young Americans. This is the same group that has tried for decades to take guns away from Americans. Guns that now are as important to the safety and lives of the American people as any time since the American Revolution. Perhaps, even more so.

The effort to end the Second Amendment rights of Americans can now be placed in proper perspective. Because now we can see that the long game being played out against America was to suppress its citizens by armed force. Perhaps if the authoritarian forces making the effort to remove guns had succeeded, this army that has been allowed within the country would have already struck. An unarmed population can easily be controlled by an armed force of foreigners who despise the American people and freedom. But the effort to remove guns has failed. And with a strong majority of Justices on the Supreme Court in favor of that right, the prospects of this cabal succeeding in the near future to scrap that important right are dim. Did the cabal change its plan for conquering America because of not being able to remove guns? Did it shift to needing a large foreign army introduced into America, ready to attack when the order comes?

The action of a government allowing an enemy army to enter its own nation is an act of treason on a scale that is not recorded in world history. It pales in comparison to the Vichy Government of France that cooperated with Nazi Germany after France was defeated in 1940. It is an act of unmatched infamy. And due to the likely massive size of the foreign army now gathered within North America, the number of innocent civilian casualties could climb into the millions before armed civilians, the U.S. military, and law enforcement can subdue the attackers and restore the nation's infrastructure.

In the scripture at the beginning of the chapter, one of the notable character traits that will be prevalent as the end times approach is that of "traitors." And for it to be included in the scriptural rendition means notable "traitors." It is difficult to be more notably involved in treason than to be vested with the responsibility of protecting a nation and to then allow an enemy army to enter it. In fact, making every effort possible to prevent others from stopping the invasion.

No doubt the first act of treason is the hardest. Thereafter, it gets easier. Perhaps what can be considered the first act of treason was turning the justice system on its head to go after the leader of the opposition party. Mr. Obama accomplishing this by placing unethical and immoral individuals in top positions of the Department of Justice and the FBI. Political activists who methodically ignore the criminal activity of those in charge of allowing the invasion, but who level false charges against those trying to stop it. Completely destroying the rule of law. Such actions are easy for individuals willing to allow their nation to be invaded. Which explains much that has been happening.

There has been a sense in recent years that certain leaders have had their loyalty to America replaced with loyalty to the international community. By that, I mean an international entity that appears to have evolved over the last hundred years and that has great power over the direction of nations, especially those in the west. The books supporting this observation are too numerous to be mentioned. The most popular name given to this force controlling nations is the New World Order. An entity without morals or ethics that controls nations from within through leaders it helped place in power. Replacing their loyalty to their own nation with loyalty to this international cabal. Whatever the reason those in power are allowing a foreign army to enter the United States, this perspective is my own conclusion.

An enemy army has now gathered within the borders of the nation. Not by splashing ashore by landing ship tanks, or dropping in by airplanes, or riding armored personal carriers across the border, but allowed in by individuals with the keys to America's gates but whose loyalty is not to America.

What has happened to America has also taken place in Europe. In France, that leader has allowed a massive number of Muslims into his country, demanding their religion be respected. But when the Olympic Games were held in Paris, he approved its opening ceremony to mock Jesus' last supper. A slap in the face to traditional European religion. But protection to a religion that kills those who criticize it. In Great Britian, thousands of its citizens have protested the mass influx of foreigners into their country. Causing crime to skyrocket and the sense of national unity to dissolve. Yet, as migrant gangs rampage across the nation, the government only reacts against native protestors labeling them "right-wing extremists."

As will shortly be presented, the prophet Isaiah foretold this invasion of America and Western Europe long ago. In one of his many prophecies, he said that those "from a far country" will enter nations they are destined to bring great destruction to. But his prophecy does not stop there. He goes on to indicate the reaction of those attacked as well as what eventually happens to the army that gathered within. And, most ominously, he tells us what prophetic time frame these events take place. To appreciate the time frame, he provided it is necessary to gain a basic but simplistic truth concerning the end times and the technical term "the day of the Lord."

What the next chapter will establish is that the Biblical technical term for the end times is that of the day of the Lord. This is important to understand because within Isaiah's prophecy he makes it clear that just before the day of the Lord the invaders begin coming into the nations, they are destined to make war with. To appreciate this requires a basic understanding of the day of the Lord.

5

ESTABLISHING THE
TIME FRAME

The event Isaiah describes, wherein nations are flooded with those "from a far country," takes place prior to the beginning of the day of the Lord. That phrase, "the day of the Lord," is the technical Biblical term used to describe what is popularly called the end times. Isaiah also identifies the attack as occurring at the beginning of the day of the Lord. This means that those "from a far country" must begin gathering within nations destined to be attacked prior to the day of the Lord starting. That is prior to the end times starting. So, it is critical to understand two things. First, that the day of the Lord is the end times from start to finish. Secondly, that we can identify the literal beginning point of the day of the Lord. Both of those ideas will now be supported.

In 1 Thessalonians 5:1-3, Paul informs us that when the day of the Lord starts, it will come suddenly. Part of what this means is that when those "from a far country" attack, it will come suddenly. And this makes sense. It will all start with a surprise attack like the attack on Pearl Harbor in December 1941. Consider the verses in question. Note the references to "the day of the Lord," and how it comes with "sudden destruction," and the application of a birth pangs reference.

> [1]But concerning the times and the seasons, brethren, you have no need that I should write to you. [2]For you yourselves know perfectly that the day of the Lord so comes as a thief in the night. [3]For when they say, "Peace and safety!" then sudden destruction comes upon them, as labor pains upon a pregnant woman. And they shall not escape. 1 Thessalonians 5:1-3

Paul tells us that when the day of the Lord starts, it brings "sudden destruction." He is talking about how the day of the Lord begins. Then he provides a birth pangs reference to describe the specific prophetic time frame of the day of the Lord (end times) with the words, "as labor pains upon a pregnant woman." The Greek word to depict birth pangs is "odin" which means of childbirth. Keep in mind Paul is not the author of these words. The Holy Spirit is guiding his writing hand and mind. The point is that the use of a birth pangs term identifies the beginning of the end times. And this is not by chance. It is a willful description provided by the Holy Spirit.

It is generally accepted that prophetic birth pangs take place at the beginning of what are called the end times. They birth something. Which means they start something. They do not take place at the midpoint or the end of the end times. Jesus reinforces that birth pangs are the beginning in His Olivet Discourse. In Matthew 24:7-8, when Jesus describes the "beginning of sorrows," once again

it is the Greek word "odin" being used to convey the "beginning."
He is confirming that a birth pangs reference is used to identify the
"beginning." We can understand that birth pangs and "beginning"
are interchangeable. End time birth pangs are the "beginning" and
the "beginning," is birth pangs. Consider His words.

> [7] For nation will rise against nation, and kingdom
> against kingdom. And there will be famines, pes-
> tilences, and earthquakes in various places. [8] All
> these are the beginning of sorrows. Matthew 24:7-8

The beginning of sorrows Jesus describes here must be the sudden destruction Paul describes in 1 Thessalonians 5:1-3. Because
both Jesus and Paul describe it as the beginning by use of the same
Greek "odin." And what Jesus describes appears to be the sudden beginning of a great world war with nations rising against one another.
The fact they must "rise" reflects the "sudden destruction" Paul
describes. Since Paul describes his "sudden destruction" as marking
the beginning of the day of the Lord, what Jesus is describing here
must also be the beginning of the day of the Lord. The end times.
Now here is a point of confusion to avoid.

In the prior verse, Matthew 24:6, Jesus describes a condition
just prior to the launch of the day of the Lord. Wherein He informs
us: "And you will hear of wars and rumors of wars. See that you are
not troubled; for all these things must come to pass, but the end
is not yet." There is a tendency to blend verse 6 with verse 7. But a
careful reading of both verses' rules that out. About the events in
verse 6 we are told not to be "troubled" and that "the end" has not
yet begun. Jesus goes out of His way to make certain we understand
this is not yet the beginning. So don't be troubled during this time.

Where verse 7 is distinguished as the "beginning of sorrows." Now consider something else about verse 7 that is notable, and it relates to Revelation Chapter 6.

Revelation 6 is the first chapter in the Book of Revelation wherein the terrible events we associate with the end times begin unfolding in all their devastation. That chapter includes the four horsemen of the apocalypse and an array of terrible events. A study comparing the descriptions of events listed in Matthew 24:7 finds all of them included in Revelation 6. The main difference is that of a single verse from Matthew 24 compared to an entire chapter in Revelation 6, which provides much more detail.

The point is that the beginning of the destructive events of the end times in Revelation 6 matches the "beginning of sorrows" found in Matthew 24:7-8. Which means Revelation 6 must also be the beginning of the day of the Lord, which is the beginning of what is popularly called the end times. The Holy Spirit is consistent. Now consider that it is still the day of the Lord at the end of the end times when Jesus steps foot on the Mount of Olives in His second coming. Which informs us that the day of the Lord is the end times from start to finish. We found this final act in Zachariah 14.

> **Behold, the day of the LORD is coming,**
> And your spoil will be divided in your midst.
> ² For I will gather all the nations to battle against Jerusalem;
> The city shall be taken,
> The houses rifled,
> And the women ravished.
> Half of the city shall go into captivity,

But the remnant of the people shall not be cut off
from the city.
³ Then the LORD will go forth
And fight against those nations,
As He fights in the day of battle.
⁴ **And in that day His feet will stand on the
Mount of Olives,**
Which faces Jerusalem on the east.
And the Mount of Olives shall be split in two,
From east to west,
Making a very large valley;
Half of the mountain shall move toward the north
And half of it toward the south.

It is still the day of the Lord when the Lord's feet stand on the Mount of Olives. Since the beginning of what we call the end times is the beginning of the day of the Lord, as identified by the use of a birth pangs reference, and it is still the day of the Lord at the end of the end times wherein Jesus steps onto the Mount of Olives, then what we call the end times is the day of the Lord from start to finish.

This understanding of the day of the Lord just provided was necessary to appreciate Isaiah's warning. Because as you will see he identifies the time frame of when nations are attacked from within by those "from a far country." As you will also see he then informs us that the same group of fighters must then flee back to their own countries as people in the attacked nations hunt them down. This is because Isaiah identifies the time frame of this happening as that of the day of the Lord. He then specifically identifies it as happening in the beginning of the day of the Lord by use of a birth pangs reference. With that information it is clearly understood that the events he describes take place at the beginning of the end times. And this means that the foreign armies must begin gathering within the nations to be attacked prior to the end times beginning. Which adds a truly ominous note to the entire invasion both America and Western Europe have experienced.

You will notice in the first three verses that Isaiah begins by describing events that took place in ancient Babylon. Do not be thrown off by that. He then immediately turns to the day of the Lord. This initial reference to ancient Babylon is made as a comparison of sorts between events that happened long ago to what is coming. Now Isaiah's warning.

6

CHAPTER

ISAIAH'S WARNING

To more fully appreciate the prophetic significance of the massive invasion at the southern border of the United States, we turn to the prophet Isaiah. His words in Chapter 13 relay a scene at the beginning of the end times that requires an invasion of nations by foreigners before it can unfold. People from across the world entering countries they are destined to attack in fulfillment of his words. Which is exactly what is now unfolding at the southern border of the United States. The massive invasion of Europe also adds to the case that the entire affair of western nations suffering these invasions is part of a plan of global conquest. Specifically directed against the West. We will begin in Isaiah 13:1-3.

In the beginning of Isaiah 13, the Lord relays an event that took place long ago involving ancient Babylon. But do not be thrown off by that. He then quickly transitions to the day of the Lord. This reference to Babylon is done to convey a similarity

- 40 -

between what transpired long ago and what is coming during the end times.

> [1]The burden against Babylon which Isaiah the son of Amoz saw.
> [2] "Lift up a banner on the high mountain, Raise your voice to them;
> Wave your hand, that they may enter the gates of the nobles.
> [3] I have commanded My sanctified ones;
> I have also called My mighty ones for My anger—
> Those who rejoice in My exaltation." Isaiah 13

Due to His anger, the Lord calls His mighty ones. And these mighty ones are a burden against ancient Babylon. After briefly mentioning that event in the distant past, He then turns His attention to the future. A dire prophecy that is unfolding in our day. The Lord musters an army for battle. And notice where they are gathering before they attack.

> [4] The noise of a multitude in the mountains,
> Like that of many people!
> A tumultuous noise of the kingdoms of nations gathered together!
> The Lord of hosts musters
> The army for battle. Isaiah 4

There is a multitude assembling in the mountains. The mountains are a place for hiding. They are gathering until the time for the attack arrives. It is a large multitude, like that of many people! But whose multitude is this? The Lord of Hosts musters the army for battle. It is a hidden army being gathered and strengthened for war. And this makes sense since it is an army that gathers within nations that are to be attacked. The fact that they gather in the mountains refers to their hiding the fact that they are a literal army within nations waiting for the order to attack. The armies gathering within America are literally hiding from sight!

> **⁵ They come from a far country,**
> From the end of heaven—
> The LORD and His weapons of indignation,
> To destroy the whole land. Isaiah 5

The army that gathers consists of those who come **from a far country.** Even from the end of heaven. But do not be thrown off by that colorful phrase involving heaven. It is used in Scripture to denote from across the globe and not heaven proper. Examples of this usage are found in Ne. 1:8-9, Dan. 8:8-9, and Jer. 49:36. Since Scripture should be used to interpret Scripture, we will accept that the army is being gathered from across the world. Exactly what has been happening since Mr. Biden took power in 2021 with military aged single men from China, Africa and the Middle East suddenly beginning to flood across the border. So those who will be used to destroy the whole land come **from a far country.** In other words, they have come within the borders of the nations they are destined to attack. They represent a literal army gathering within those nations. Hiding themselves as an army in the proverbial mountains.

In verse 4 we are told "the Lord of Hosts musters the army for battle." Verse 5 describes it as "The LORD and His weapons of indignation, to destroy the whole land." What is clear is that this army gathering within nations is being used by the Lord. The Lord uses the wicked to do His will. In this case to literally bring destruction against nations who once followed Him but then turned to other gods. Forgetting the true God of heaven Who kept them safe and prosperous. And as is so common in relationships, great trials bring people back to their senses. And the trial about to strike America will be the greatest in her history.

Then the Lord identifies the prophetic time frame for when they will attack.

> ⁶ Wail, for **the day of the LORD** is at hand!
> It will come as destruction from the Almighty.
> ⁷ Therefore all hands will be limp,
> Every man's heart will melt. Isaiah 13

It is the day of the Lord. The time when God's wrath is unleashed upon the world for its sin. This sin includes removing some land from Israel in the name of Peace. A false Peace — another major sign coming shortly before the end times launch. The land in question is that which the Lord long ago foretold would be restored to a reconstituted state of Israel. And it was in 1948 when Israel came back into the land as a nation again. Fulfilling an amazing prophecy.

This is why those who gather within nations can become an army hiding in the "mountains." Not literally in the mountains. Isaiah is telling us that citizens within the invaded nations will not realize that an actual army is forming within their borders. Because they are the Lord's weapons of indignation, to destroy the whole land, they remain hidden until the order to attack comes. Is such a calamity coming to America and the west because of widespread abortion? Even wanting to kill the baby outside the womb. Is it because America led the way in defiling God's institution of marriage? Is it because America leads the world in pornography? Is this judgment coming against America because a large segment of the nation has set out to be enemies of God?

Is America saved in the end because of all the Christians who for many years traveled the world to bring the gospel to every corner as well as praying for his favor over America? Is the coming great war on American soil what it takes to return America to Him? Although we cannot be certain of the answers to these questions, one thing we do know. Armies are gathering within America just as foretold by Isaiah.

But simply knowing this event will take place during the day of the Lord, although that is helpful, we still need more information. We need to know when during the day of the Lord these armies launch their attack. Blessed be the Lord, for He tells us.

> [8]And they will be afraid.
> Pangs and sorrows will take hold of them;
> **They will be in pain as a woman in childbirth**;
> They will be amazed at one another;
> Their faces will be like flames. Isaiah 13

It is during birth pangs, the beginning phase of the day of the Lord. We know this from the use of the phrase "As a woman in childbirth." In the Old Testament, the Hebrew word "yalad" is used for birth pangs. This identifies the time frame within which the devastating attack by those "from a far country" will take place. It is part of the opening scene of the great war that launches the end times. Of all the armies of the world that engage in combat at the sudden start of the day of the Lord, certain armies are those that secretly gathered within nations. Why has this approach of hiding an army within certain nations been taken? Because nations as strong militarily as the United States and Western Europe cannot be conquered from an external direct attack. But when an army of several hundred thousand is already within its borders, even a very strong nation can be brought to its knees. By attacking from within, the military strength of America and Western Europe is nullified.

In the *The Sixth King*, it is pointed out that the Antichrist has mastery of deception. He is described as the master of both "dark sentences" as well as "craft." Meaning he can devise deceptive plans and plots beyond the ability of any leader in world history. In this respect, he is in a league with himself. From a purely military standpoint, the assembly of an army within enemy nations is brilliant. Such a military feat has only been possible after decades of indoctrination. Especially at so-called universities. Institutions that once provided higher education were slowly transformed into expensive indoctrination camps. What entity has been behind this over the course of decades? The New World Order. Within *The Sixth King* is presented the case that the Beast Kingdom in its final Biblical form has existed since around the year 1900 in what has become known as the New World Order. That is not to say elements of it have not existed for prior centuries. No doubt they have.

As the reader can see, for these events of Isaiah 13 to unfold as foretold, there had be a period of wide-open borders. Allowing time for the armies to gather within their soon-to-be victims' nations. This is a prophecy unfolding before the eyes of the church. And it happens just before the end time's launch. Now Isaiah provides more detail concerning those who attack as well as the reaction of the people within nations after the attack begins. He also tells us about the response of those from a far country thereafter. But to gain proper perspective, it is first necessary to appreciate how devastating the opening wars of the end times will be.

When studying the beginning scene of the day of the Lord, it wreaks devastation. The Joel 3:2, we are told the Lord gathers nations for judgment in the Valley of Jehoshaphat, a term used for the theater of God's judgment against "all nations" in both the opening scene of the end times as well as the final judgment at the Battle of Armageddon. In Jeremiah 30, which has a birth pangs reference relative to the day of the Lord, the prophet tells of all nations being made a full end. In other words, they are devastated. Isaiah tells us this opening scene will destroy the whole land. In the Book of Revelation we see the four horsemen of the Apocalypse bringing great devastation. The devastation wrought by those horsemen is a description of the birth pangs devastation mentioned by Jesus in Matthew 24: 7-8, where nations rise against each other. But it is in 2 Peter 3 where there appears to be a reference to the use of nuclear weapons.

> [10] But the day of the Lord will come as a thief in the night, in which the heavens will pass away with a great noise, and the elements will melt with fervent heat; both the earth and the works that are in it will be burned up. 2 Peter 3

When nuclear weapons detonate, there is a great noise, and the elements will melt with fervent heat. This is the opening scene of the day of the Lord from the usage of the phrase that it will "come as a thief in the night." This is the exact same phrase used in 1 Thessalonians 5:1-3, which describes the sudden beginning of the day of the Lord as birth pangs. Is the army entering the United States through the open southern border bringing with them suitcase nuclear weapons?

Having described in vivid detail how devastating the opening scene of the day of the Lord is, there is now context for the reaction of people within the nations struck by those from a far country. And keep in mind that America is a nation with hundreds of millions of guns in the hands of its people. Providing them with the ability to defend themselves against an internal attack. Which provides the means to eventually turn the tide. As a result, the foreign army becomes the hunted and must flee back to their own lands.

> [14] It shall be as the hunted gazelle,
> And as a sheep that no man takes up;
> Every man will turn to his own people,
> And everyone will flee to his own land.

A gazelle being hunted will flee. But sheep are more vulnerable. Without protection they are easy prey. And those from a far country — even if they had nothing to do with the opening attack — will be as a sheep that no man takes up to protect. Many are completely vulnerable to retaliation for the attack, whether innocent or guilty. As a result of this retaliation, every man will turn to his own people. To save the lives of themselves and their families, everyone will flee to his own land. America will become a land of deadly hostility for those from a far country who brought devastation to its shores. Then more details of why they must flee back to their lands of origin.

> [15] Everyone who is found will be thrust through,
> And everyone who is captured will fall by the sword.
> [16] Their children also will be dashed to pieces before
> their eyes;
> Their houses will be plundered
> And their wives ravished. Isaiah 13

It will be a time of mass killings in America. First, the foreign army will devastate American cities. Then, without an organized government able to restore order, the rage of a heavily armed civilian population who have suffered great loss of life and betrayal will take matters into their own hands. And with devastating effects. Everyone who is found will be killed. Everyone who is captured will be killed. Even their children will not be spared. Their homes will be plundered, as will their wives. It will be a time of mayhem, death, and destruction. If ever there was any doubt that it is those coming in from other lands who bring destruction, acting as an army within the borders of the United States and Western Europe, the reaction of both the attackers and the attacked resolves any doubts.

As all of this is happening in America, it is but a part of a much larger picture unfolding across the world. This attack on America (and Western Europe) takes place at the opening scene of the end times. As the master of craft and dark sentences, the Antichrist is also directly attacking armies of nations as well as nations from within with his armies that have been gathering. His ability to massively attack nations from within represents a historical master stroke never before done. It will be a morbid first in world history. Enabled by treasonous elements within morally compromised nations. Here is something else concerning the Antichrist. A mystery that is now resolved.

THE RIDER OF THE WHITE HORSE

As we looked at Revelation 6 is the first chapter in that apocalyptic book that the horrific events, we associate with the end times begin unfolding. It is there that the four-horsemen of the apocalypse begin their devastating ride. But there has always been a mystery of sorts concerning the first rider who is released by the first seal. That is the rider of the white horse. Of all the horsemen released by the undoing of the four seals, it is the white horse who does not appear to be that dangerous. And yet most people who study Bible prophecy have concluded that this rider is the Antichrist. Consider the verses.

> Now I saw when the Lamb opened one of the seals; and I heard one of the four living creatures saying with a voice like thunder, "Come and see." And I looked, and behold, a white horse. He who sat on it had a bow; and a crown was given to him, and he went out conquering and to conquer.

There are many theories on the rider of the white horse. Most have him as the Antichrist, which I agree with. And since he has no arrows, most have explained this by assuming that he is conquering through peace. And this makes sense. But by fully appreciating the unfolding of Isaiah's prophecy, wherein nations experience enemy armies entering through borders left wide open by treasonous elements, there now appears to be a much better answer as to why he has no arrows but only a bow. And yet succeeds in going about conquering and to conquer.

Isaiah 13 adds that in addition to national armies fighting one another on fields of battle, there will also be great fronts opened within nations themselves attacked from within. The Antichrist will be responsible for those attacks because he has the bow that directs them. Yet, the actual attacks or arrows cannot be traced back to him because they are an internal army hiding in the mountains. Thus, he conquers with only a bow. How will people be able to say who controls the army attacking their towns and cities? Because it comes from within. An army made up of Middle Easterners, Africans, and Chinese. Who will they be able to identify as the leader who controls these armies, destroying their infrastructure and causing all power to be cut off.

The point is that the real leader who controls the army will likely remain unknown. That is until an international leader comes forward who is able to make peace. That will be the Antichrist. This is why he has a bow but no arrows. The bow is used to direct attacks. But those attacks (arrows) cannot be traced back to him. He will look like a peace maker when he is a monster bringing death and destruction on a mass scale.

It is important to understand that the Antichrist will be the master of "craft" and "dark sentences." This is why he attacks nations in ways never thought of previously. And then he will make himself look like a savior. From a dark perspective it is brilliant. But despite his dark brilliance, it may be that America eventually is set free based on Isaiah and also the words of Daniel.

7

DANIEL TO THE RESCUE OF AMERICA?

There is a prophecy in the Book of Daniel (Chapter 7), which uses animal symbolism in depicting various nations. It is called the lion, leopard, and bear prophecy. There is good reason to believe that America is included in this prophecy. To follow along, let me explain the approach this chapter will take. First, you will be provided with some background on the lion, leopard and bear by looking at Revelation 13. Then you will be given what is currently the most accepted perspective on the prophecy. Then it will be presented why that dominant perspective appears to be ruled out by other words of Daniel. And finally, a more reasonable explanation of what Daniel is conveying by using the symbolism of a lion, leopard, and bear and why it may involve the nations of Great Britain, Russia, Germany, and America. Additionally, this perspective fits better with Isaiah 13 than the dominant one. So read with care to follow the points being made.

Within the first verses of Revelation 13, there is a mysterious beast described in terms that are both strange and fearsome. It is a twisted and freakish entity better suited for the winding and fiery caverns of hell than the earth. It is a beast the like of which has never been seen until it rises from the sea of politics, with the help of the dragon, its blasphemies going before it in a plague of sin and death across the entire earth. This is the Beast Kingdom being described as possessing three distinct characteristics. It is the part describing the lion, leopard, and bear that has our attention. Here is the description provided in Revelation 13.

> Then I stood on the sand of the sea. And I saw a beast rising up out of the sea, having seven heads and ten horns, and on his horns ten crowns, and on his heads a blasphemous name. [2] **Now the beast which I saw was like a leopard, his feet were like the feet of a bear, and his mouth like the mouth of a lion.** The dragon gave him his power, his throne, and great authority. Revelation 13

The Antichrist Beast Kingdom is described in mysterious terms as having seven heads, ten horns, and the appearance of a lion, leopard, and a bear. In *The End of the Age*, all three are dissected for the role they play in the Beast Kingdom. Each has a clear meaning when using other Scriptures to break them down into understandable parts. But considering the lion, leopard, and bear, the most reasonable reading of what they represent is animal symbolism of nations that did not exist at the time Daniel was given the prophecy but would be in play at the time of the end. With each playing a significant role during the end times.

THE LION, LEOPARD, AND
THE BEAR PROPHECY

In dissecting the strange creature from the sea, we find that the beast has friends. Better to say, accomplices. And, of course, they are presented in mystery form. Mysteries abound when it comes to the beast kingdom. In addition to the seven heads and ten horns, the beast kingdom possesses the characteristics of a lion, leopard, and bear.

Who else but the dragon would be behind such a distorted beast? It takes the prophet Daniel to provide critical clues as to what these animals represent. And once that is understood, then speculation as to who they are becomes possible. Consider the full descriptions of these beasts given by Daniel, which provide more detail than Revelation 13.

> ² Daniel spoke, saying, "I saw in my vision by night, and behold, the four winds of heaven were stirring up the Great Sea. ³ And four great beasts came up from the sea, each different from the other. ⁴ The **first was like a lion, and had eagle's wings**. I watched till its wings were plucked off; and it was lifted up from the earth and made to stand on two feet like a man, and a man's heart was given to it.
>
> ⁵ "**And suddenly another beast, a second, like a bear.** It was raised up on one side, and had three ribs in its mouth between its teeth. And they said thus to it: 'Arise, devour much flesh!'

> [6] **"After this I looked, and there was another, like a leopard,** which had on its back four wings of a bird. The beast also had four heads, and dominion was given to it. Daniel 7:2-6

There are "four great beasts." The fourth is the horrid Antichrist kingdom. But it is the first three we are focused on. The debate concerning those first three, the lion, leopard, and bear, centers on whether they are ancient kingdoms from the past, or if they will be contemporary major allies of the Antichrist. And the issue can be easily resolved thanks to Daniel.

THE DOMINANT INTERPRETATION

Those who consider these beasts as relics of the past link them to the kingdoms described in the prophecy of Daniel 2. They believe the lion, leopard, and bear symbolize the ancient realms of Babylon, Media-Persia, and Greece. In Daniel 2, these ancient kingdoms are depicted as parts of a statue seen by King Nebuchadnezzar in a dream—Babylon, for instance, is portrayed as the statue's head. Consequently, from this viewpoint, their significance for future events is minimal. And it should be noted that if they were ancient kingdoms, then they would not be involved in any way during the end times. Obviously, there would certainly be no need for the Lord to punish them during the end times. However, Daniel 7 offers a passage that challenges this dominant interpretation.

> [11]"I watched then because of the sound of the pompous words which the horn was speaking; I watched till the beast was slain, and its body destroyed and

given to the burning flame. **¹² As for the rest of the beasts, they had their dominion taken away, yet their lives were prolonged for a season and a time.** Daniel 7:11-12

Daniel begins by detailing the fate of the Antichrist, the "fourth beast," emphasizing the fiery destruction of this figure and his kingdom. This event takes place at the end of the end times. So, if the lion, leopard, and bear are from the distant past, then they should not be dealt with here as well. But they are. Although not explicitly named, we recognize this as the Battle of Armageddon. Because we know the Antichrist and his Beast Kingdom meet their end in that final battle. Notably, in the same passage, the fate of the other "beasts"—the lion, leopard, and bear—is also described. While the ferocious Antichrist is condemned to eternal fire, the other three beasts meet a different end: their dominion is stripped away, yet their lives are prolonged for a season and a time. This clearly indicates that they will exist during the time of the Antichrist and his Beast Kingdom, dismissing the notion that they were mere echoes of a distant past. They are contemporaries of the Antichrist's kingdom, punished alongside him, with their dominion taken away as he is cast into the fire.

As the beast kingdom is dissolved into the ash heap of history, the lives of the lion, leopard, and bear continue but without dominion. They are allowed to outlive the Antichrist for a time. Since the lion, leopard, and bear are clearly separate powers from the Antichrist kingdom, but aligned with it and facing a similar fate, this description of the final disposition of all four beasts makes it clear that the lion, leopard, and bear appear to be major allied nations of the dark Antichrist kingdom. Like what Italy and Japan represented to the odious Nazi regime of the 1930s and 40s. Otherwise, why would they be getting punished along with the Antichrist Beast Kingdom?

But sometimes wrong teachings die a stubborn death. And the notion that the lion, leopard, and bear are from the ancient past is one of them. As mentioned earlier, that theory has those three beasts as ancient Babylon, Media-Persia, and Greece. Which would eliminate their significance to America, which we will shortly look at. However, consider that Daniel 8 rules out ancient Media-Persia and Greece from being any part of these beasts. And places a dagger in the heart of the ancient kingdom theory.

> [20] The **ram** which you saw, having the two horns— they are the kings of **Media and Persia**. [21] And the male **goat** is the kingdom of **Greece**. The large horn that is between its eyes is the first king. Daniel 8:20-21

In Daniel 8, we are told that the ancient kingdoms of Media/Persia and Greece have specific animal symbolism associated with them. The "ram" for Media/Persia and the "goat" for Greece. This rules out the possibility that either can be the lion, leopard, or bear in the previous chapter. Otherwise, it is necessary to believe the Holy Spirit used one set of animal symbolism in chapter 7 and then changed them in chapter 8 when speaking about the same kingdoms. Which should be a bridge too far to cross for anyone who respects the consistency of God.

All of this makes it very probable that these three beasts in Chapter 7 are contemporary major allies of the Antichrist kingdom. Now the question arises as to which nations they refer to at the time this prophecy will be fulfilled. Since the nations are not specifically identified in the way Daniel 8 identifies ancient Media-Persia and Greece, then we are relegated to logical speculation. One reason they may not be specifically identified is because the nation-states they represent did not exist at the time the prophecy was given. Therefore, animal symbolism was used so they could later be identified when their time arrived. Because there is a tendency to impart certain animal symbolism to nations.

Bible prophecy is informative. And for the information concerning these three beasts to be informative, the animal depictions used should have meaning in the present day. Since these allies are noted in prophecy multiple times, we should believe they will be major allies. So, the nations they depict should have notable standing and power relative to the vast array of nations on the earth today. If they were insignificant allies, then they would not warrant so much Biblical attention. And this alone eliminates many candidate nations.

In the modern age, certain animals are used to depict various nations. The roar of the British lion was heard around the world at one time. It was even said that the sun never set on its territory. Although their empire is now history, the use of the lion to depict Great Britain is not. As for the bear there is this. During the cold war there was a Time magazine cover that pitted the bear against the eagle. The bear, of course, was Russia, and the eagle was the United States. Those animals were used for the two countries because they are generally accepted in the current day as symbolic of both. As for the leopard, that one is not clear. Some speculate it is Germany and it may be. Certainly, Germany is a major nation today.

Accordingly, if the animal symbolism used by Daniel is meant to identify these major nations allied with the Antichrist at the time his ungodly kingdom is on earth, then they appear to be identifiable. Additionally, since the lion has eagle's wings that are plucked off then, it would appear the United States is also mentioned. And one solid geopolitical fact in the modern age is that the United States and Great Britain are the closest of allies. So, the lion having eagle wings may very well indicate the closeness of both nations. Based on these observations, here is what we see.

Great Britain aligns with the savage Antichrist kingdom. And considering the massive Muslim population now in that island nation that is not unreasonable. At the time they do so, the United States is still firmly attached to the old alliance with them. This would appear to be the case because at the time the lion joins with the Antichrist, the eagle's wings are still attached. But then we are told, "I watched till its wings were plucked off." Perhaps a leader in the U.S. led by the Lord will end the United States-Britain alliance at that point. If so, then the United States would also be breaking away from the Antichrist kingdom.

Some speculate that the eagle's wings breaking off from the lion is symbolic of the American Revolutionary War. Wherein the fledgling American colonies broke away from the mother country. Although the animal symbolism is right for both countries, that reading is unlikely accurate since scripture is describing the condition of these Antichrist allies at the time they partner with him and not some time frame in their past. And the eagle's wings are with Britain as the lion enters the pit of darkness to join the Antichrist. All of this is completely based on the lion representing Great Britain and the eagle's wings representing the United States.

Based on this perspective, there are various political realities inferred. The sudden removal of the eagle's wings would seem to indicate that the close alliance between Great Britain and the United

States will come to an abrupt halt. But also, that the United States may enter a kind of fortress America-type isolation in an attempt to avoid the far-reaching and powerful tentacles of the Antichrist empire. However, considering what Isaiah 13 tells us, America will be consumed with defeating the foreign armies allowed within the nation. Even after driving them out, it is likely that the level of destruction across the country will be such that the nation will be self-consumed with rebuilding for a period. It will also take time to locate the treasonous elements that remain in the country after America wins her second war for independence.

The other possibility is that the U.S. will go into active opposition against the Antichrist. The fact that the United States is initially alongside Britain in alliance with the Antichrist opens the possibility of a White House initially darkened by a black shadow. But the abrupt removal of the eagle's wings may indicate the Lord freeing America from this dark grip. It also indicates a right-of-center government in charge in the United States. This is because any left-of-center government, currently referred to as "progressive" (an oxymoron term), would embrace the Antichrist due to their common anti-God beliefs. But there is another possibility.

As detailed in *The End of the Age*, after the great destruction of all nations during the birth pangs beginning of the day of the Lord, both the United States and Great Britain, having experienced Jeremiah's full end, are incapable of resisting the Antichrist who rides the white horse of Revelation 6 during that time to take over the world. Whereas Great Britain remains under his boot for the duration of the end times, the United States breaks free from his wicked grasp. Possibly because of the hundreds of millions of firearms spread out across the vast North American continent. As previously mentioned, wherein America is eventually set free is in line with Isaiah telling us that those "from a far country" must flee back to their own lands.

What is interesting is that this scenario indicating America is invaded by peoples from across the world and then engaged in a great war, which it eventually wins, has been repeated long ago in American folklore. Or, perhaps, it is more than folklore. It was reported in the 1800s that George Washington experienced a vision while spending the winter at Valley Forge. A vision the essence of which is now playing out exactly as indicated.

8

WASHINGTON'S VISION

We know from the prophet Joel that the Lord gives men prophetic dreams and visions. This is not to say these messages from God add to scripture. They do not. When the Lord provides prophetic knowledge, it is on events yet to happen. Consider Joel's words.

> "And it shall come to pass afterward
> That I will pour out My Spirit on all flesh;
> Your sons and your daughters shall prophesy,
> Your old men shall dream dreams,
> Your young men shall see visions. Joel 2:28

As the Lord's Spirit is poured out on all flesh, it will deliver prophecy knowledge to them in the form of dreams and visions. Of course, the church must use great discernment as to which prophetic claims from individuals are true and which are false.

It is unusual for a ministry that takes scripture very literally to include a prophetic vision from a man. But a rare exception needs to be made for a vision that George Washington reportedly experienced while encamped for the winter at Valley Forge. The reason for this exception is threefold. The first is that Scripture tells us that men can receive prophetic visions from the Lord. As Joel indicates, He delivers those prophetic messages using dreams or visions. The second reason this exception is being made is the historical evidence indicating that Washington had the Lord's protection throughout the Revolutionary War. More on that in a moment. And lastly, and most importantly, the vision he reportedly experienced is unfolding in complete detail over two-hundred years later! The odds of that happening by chance have to be very small.

I understand some will question the wisdom of including any man's vision here. If I were not writing this, I would likely be in that camp. But the grand events Washington was involved in during the war altered the course of world history. The multiple reports of some form of Divine protection over him in the heat of battle are well documented. And we know there is no real protection outside of the Lord, which seems to confirm that the Lord was with him.

WASHINGTON'S DIVINE PROTECTION

It is reported that Washington would encourage his men to fight during the Revolutionary War by riding his white steed in front of their line of fire to instill the courage he was exhibiting in each of them. However, this demonstration provided the enemy with a clear shot at him. Although this placed him in great danger, he was never struck by a single bullet. Then there is the French and Indian War.

During a battle in that war, Washington became the target of an Indian riflemen. Riding his horse in front of his troops he appeared to make an easy target. Amazingly, he was not hit. One of the Indian warriors, a leader of his tribe, years later recounted the efforts to shoot Washington. Saying, "Washington was never born to be killed by a bullet! I had seventeen fair fires at him with my rifle, and after all, could not bring him to the ground!" Later, writing to his brother, Washington would relay his account of that same battle.

> "As I have heard since my arrival at this place, a circumstantial account of my death and dying speech, I take this early opportunity of contradicting the first and of assuring you that I have not as yet composed the latter. But by the all-powerful dispensations of Providence I have been protected beyond all human probability or expectation; for I had four bullets through my coat, and two horses shot under me yet escaped unhurt, although death was leveling my companions on every side of me!"

Whether or not Divine protection was at work is for you to decide. However, the reported vision Washington is claimed to have experienced is amazing if for no other reason than it is unfolding. At least the stage is being set for it to unfold because of the mass invasion. His vision includes three great trials that America would go through. The first was the Revolutionary War of which he was actively engaged in fighting at the time the vision was given. The second clearly appears to be the Civil War. Startlingly, the third is that America will be invaded from Asia, Africa (Middle East) and Europe by armies that would gather within the nation. Bringing great destruction. That gathering is exactly what started happening immediately after Mr. Biden took power.

Some claim the whole vision is a work of fiction. They support that by claiming that the person who reportedly was told the vision by Washington, and then later relayed it to a writer, a soldier named Anthony Sherman, was not listed as one of Washington's soldiers at Valley Forge. And if that's where the story stood then it would not have made its way into this book.

Fortunately, there are good enough Revolutionary War records to piece together the fact that Mr. Sherman was at Valley Forge during the winter of 1777-78. We know this because Mr. Sherman applied for the Revolutionary War pension in 1831. When he did so he had to complete a lengthy application describing in detail his activities during the war. In other words, we have documentation of his war record. And at that time the U.S. government did substantial due diligence to verify the accuracy of all applications before releasing funds to the old soldiers.

Mr. Sherman's application states that in the fall of 1777 he was in a regiment under the command of Col. Henry B. Livingston. Historically, we know that Col. Livingston's regiment was encamped at Valley Forge during the winter of 1777-78. Mr. Sherman then notes that in June of 1778 he fought at the Battle of Monmouth, which was Washington's first battle after the winter at Valley Forge ended. Which means that Mr. Sherman was not only at Valley Forge during the time General Washington was there, but that when his regiment came out of Valley Forge after the harsh winter, it went on to fight with Washington in June of 1778.

This detail and much more is provided online by the ministry Bible Scribe. And a link to the online site with all documentation is provided at the end of this chapter. This evidence is necessary to debunk the "fact checkers" who have clearly got it wrong. Although the fact that Mr. Sherman was at Valley Forge does not prove Washington told him about a vision, it leaves open the possibility that he did. Because we know Sherman was there. Now consider Washington's reported vision and the uncanny way it corresponds to the Revolutionary War, Civil War, and the invasion of enemy forces from around the world entering the United States. Ultimately to launch a great war on American soil. Then decide if you believe this is only a coincidence.

GEORGE WASHINGTON'S VALLEY FORGE VISION

The earliest report of "Washington's vision" able to be found was recorded by Wesley Bradshaw in the *National Tribune*, Vol. 4, No. 12, December 1880. Later the name of the *National Tribune* was changed to the *Stars and Stripes*. This does not mean there was not an even earlier version.

> The last time I ever saw Anthony Sherman was on July 4, 1859, in Independence Square. He was then 99 years old, and becoming very feeble. But though so old, his dimming eyes rekindled as he gazed upon Independence Hall, which he came to visit once more.
>
> "Let us go into the hall," he said. "I want to tell you an incident of Washington's life -- one which no one alive knows of except myself; and if you live, you will before long, see it verified."

"From the opening of the Revolution we experienced all phases of fortune, now good and now ill; one time victorious and another conquered. The darkest period we had, I think, was when Washington, after several reverses, retreated to Valley Forge, where he resolved to spend the winter of 1777. Ah! I have often seen our dear commander's care-worn cheeks, as he would be conversing with a confidential officer about the condition of his poor soldiers. You have doubtless heard the story of Washington's going to the thicket to pray. Well, it was not only true, but he used often to pray in secret for aid and comfort from God, the interposition of whose Divine Providence brought us safely through the darkest days of tribulation.

"One day, I remember well, the chilly winds whistled through the leafless trees, though the sky was cloudless and the sun shone brightly, he remained in his quarters nearly all the afternoon alone. When he came out, I noticed that his face was a shade paler than usual, and there seemed to be something on his mind of more than ordinary importance. Returning just after dusk, he dispatched an orderly to the quarters of the officer I mention who was presently in attendance. After a preliminary conversation of about half an hour, Washington, gazing upon his companion with that strange look of dignity which he alone could command said to the latter:

"I do not know whether it is owing to anxiety of my mind, or what, but this afternoon, as I was sitting at this table engaged in preparing a dispatch, something seemed to disturb me. Looking up, I beheld standing opposite me a singularly beautiful female. So astonished was I, for I had given strict orders not to be disturbed, that it was some moments before I found language to inquire the cause of her presence. A second, a third, and even a fourth time did I repeat my question, but received no answer from my mysterious visitor except a slight raising of her eyes.

"Presently I heard a voice saying, 'Son of the Republic, look and learn,' while at the same time my visitor extended her arm eastwardly. I now beheld a heavy white vapor at some distance rising fold upon fold. This gradually dissipated, and I looked upon a strange scene. Before me lay spread out in one vast plain all the countries of the world --Europe, Asia, Africa, and America. I saw rolling and tossing, between Europe and America, the billows of the Atlantic, and between Asia and America lay the Pacific.

"'Son of the Republic,' said the same mysterious voice as before, 'look and learn.' At that moment I beheld a dark, shadowy being, like an angel, standing, or rather floating, in the hollow air, between Europe and America. Dipping water out of the ocean in the hollow of each hand, he sprinkled some upon America with his right hand while with his left hand he cast some on Europe. Immediately a cloud raised from these countries and joined in mid-ocean. For a while it remained stationary, and then moved slowly westward, until it enveloped America in its murky folds. Sharp flashes of lightning gleamed through it at intervals, and I heard the smothered groans and cries of the American people. (Author's Note: The Revolutionary War)

"A second time the angel dipped water from the ocean, and sprinkled it out as before. The dark cloud was then drawn back to the ocean, in whose heaving billows it sank from view. A third time I heard the mysterious voice saying, 'Son of the Republic, look and learn.' I cast my eyes upon America and beheld villages and towns and cities springing up one after another until the whole land, from the Atlantic to the Pacific, was dotted with them. Again I heard the mysterious voice say, 'Son of the Republic, the end of the century cometh, look and learn.'

"At this the dark shadowy angel turned his face southward, and from Africa I saw an ill-omened specter approach our land. It flitted slowly over every town and city of the latter. The inhabitants presently set themselves in battle array against each other. As I continued looking, I saw a bright angel, on whose brow rested a crown of light, on which was traced the word 'Union,' bearing the American flag which he placed between the divided nation, and said, 'Remember ye are brethren.' Instantly, the inhabitants casting from them their weapons became friends once more, and united around the National Standard.

(Author's Note: The Civil War)

"And again I heard the mysterious voice saying, 'Son of the Republic, look and learn.' At this, the dark, shadowy angel placed a trumpet to his mouth and blew three distinct blasts; and taking water from the ocean, he sprinkled it upon Europe, Asia, and Africa. Then my eyes beheld a fearful scene. From each of these countries arose thick, black clouds that were soon joined into one. And throughout this mass, there gleamed a dark red light by which I saw hordes of armed men, who, moving with the cloud, marched by land and sailed by sea to America, which country was enveloped in the volume of cloud. And I dimly saw these vast armies devastate the whole country, and burn the villages, towns and cities that I beheld springing up.

"As my ears listened to the thundering of the cannon, clashing of swords, and the shouts and cries of millions in mortal combat., I again heard the mysterious voice saying, 'Son of the Republic, look and learn.' When the voice had ceased, the dark shadowy angel placed his trumpet once more to his mouth, and blew a long and fearful blast.

"Instantly a light as of a thousand suns shone down from above me, and pierced and broke into fragments the dark cloud which enveloped America. At the same moment the angel upon whose head still shone the word 'Union,' and who bore our national flag in one hand and a sword in the other, descended from the heavens attended by legions of white spirits. These immediately joined the inhabitants of America, who I perceived were well-nigh overcome, but who immediately taking courage again closed up their broken ranks and renewed the battle. Again, amid the fearful noise of the conflict, I heard the mysterious voice saying, 'Son of the Republic, look and learn.'

"As the voice ceased, the shadowy angel for the last time dipped water from the ocean and sprinkled it upon America. Instantly the dark cloud rolled back, together with the armies it had brought, leaving the inhabitants of the land victorious. (Author's Note: This vision points to what is currently unfolding.)

"Then once more I beheld the villages, towns and cities, springing up where I had seen them before, while the bright angel, plating the azure standard he had brought in the midst of them, cried with a loud voice: 'While the stars remain, and the heavens send down dew upon the earth, so long shall the Union last.' And taking from his brow the crown on which was blazoned the word 'Union,' he placed it upon the Standard, while the people, kneeling down, said 'Amen.'

"The scene instantly began to fade and dissolve, and I at last saw nothing but the rising, curling vapor I at first beheld. This also disappearing, I found myself once more gazing upon the mysterious visitor, who in the same voice I had heard before, said, 'Son of the Republic, what you have seen is thus interpreted. Three great perils will come upon the Republic. The most fearful is the third.'

"(The comment on his word 'third' is: 'The help against the THIRD peril comes in the shape of Divine assistance; passing which, the whole world united shall not prevail against her. Let every child of the Republic learn to live for his God, his land and Union.')

"With these words the vision vanished, and I started from my seat and felt that I had seen a vision wherein had been shown me the birth, progress, and destiny of the UNITED STATES."

"Such, my friends," concluded the venerable narrator, "were the words I heard from Washington's own lips, and America will do well to profit by them."

According to the vision, it is the third and final great war that will be the worst. Greater than the Revolutionary War and the Civil War. The forces of these armies are currently building their ranks within America.

CONCLUSION

You must decide if what is reported to be a Divine vision from Washington is true or not. But when considering the prophecy of Isaiah 13, wherein at the beginning of the end times nations are attacked from within, and then the attackers must flee back to their own lands, Washington's reported vision appears to be close to what we know is true from that prophet. And all of this raises the most obvious question. Who is behind this planned invasion of America?

(To review the evidence that Anthony Sherman was stationed at Valley Forge during the Winter of 1777-78, the following link will direct you to the account of the Bible Scribe. You will find a host of old Revolutionary War documents concerning Mr. Sherman posted for review. Kudos to him!
https://bible-scribe.com/research/george-washingtons-vision.php)

9

THE BARACK
OBAMA FACTOR

Somewhere in the highest levels of power are individuals who planned and executed the entry of a foreign army into the United States through the southern border. If those foreign military units are at least in the tens of thousands, which is very likely, then what is coming to America is unspeakable. That level of treachery is not easily found in history. Although efforts by groups and individuals to take over a country are common in world history, leaders of a country turning over their nation to a foreign army is not found anywhere in history. Yet, we are seeing that level of betrayal unfold before our eyes.

The closest modern history comes to the level of treason currently unfolding against America is that of Vidkun Quisling. He was a fascist politician from Norway who traveled to Berlin in 1939 to meet with Hitler. The purpose of the meeting was to convince

Hitler to invade his country before the British did. Prior to his meeting Hitler had not considered Norway strategically important. However, with the German war machine relying on iron ore from Norway to keep going, should the British take it over it would be a major blow to the Third Reich. In fact, Quisling was right, British Prime minister Winston Churchill was planning on that exact move. As a result, Hitler seized Norway. Since that betrayal of his country, the name Quisling has become a byword for traitor.

The planned invasion by foreign armies through the southern border should not be viewed in isolation. But rather as a larger pattern of betrayal. Such as the assassination attempt on President Trump. Shortly followed by what was effectively a coup against Mr. Biden, eliminating him from running for reelection. The turning of the Federal Bureau of Investigation and the Department of Justice into third-world weapons against the main enemy of the Democratic Party. Corruption that began unfolding only after Mr. Obama instituted changes to some of the most significant government agencies.

During his term in office, something happened to the FBI. It is reported that before Mr. Obama left office, he filled their upper ranks with Democratic Party activists. Resulting in the use of their massive power to go after political enemies. And the Department of Justice appears to have followed suit. The most glaring example of weaponizing these two agencies is found in their political actions against former President Trump. Not only have these agencies demonstrated a disregard for the rule of law on a federal level, but there appears to have been coordination with state and local District Attorney offices to join the political war against their enemy. Such actions are unheard of in American history, but not in places like Germany during the 1930s. What

Mr. Obama appears to have succeeded in doing is ripping the blindfold off lady justice.

It appears that the election of Mr. Trump in 2016 was a shock to Mr. Obama. But even before that election, his team of FBI and DOJ operatives began acting. It eventually came out that both agencies ran comprehensive surveillance operations against his campaign. A first in US history. Using this lawless campaign, they manufactured a completely fabricated case that Trump was colluding with Russia. And after his election, their corrupt practices continued.

In 2017, just as the Trump administration was getting going, the DOJ engaged a Special Counsel to investigate the falsified Russia accusations. However, what appears to be the real reason behind these attacks was to provide cover for their illegal surveillance operation against the Trump campaign. And then there were the two impeachment hoaxes. One of which was started by intelligence operatives Mary McCord and Michael Atkinson. Another corrupted agency working the will of Mr. Obama.

Perhaps the most significant policy President Trump pursued during his term in office was to begin closing the southern border, thereby greatly reducing the number of Central Americans coming through illegally. In that effort, he built a wall in those areas of the border where natural barriers did not exist. Eventually, large sections of it were put in place. But not all of it. With sections still open, it was possible for illegal entries to be successful on a large scale. But once fully completed, the illegal flow would drop to a trickle. The reelection of Mr. Trump would guarantee completion of the wall and an end to illegal immigration on any significant scale, making it impossible for those planning the invasion of America to proceed. Unless they literally began tearing down sections of the wall. An action that would have been politically impossible. This meant that for those wanting a full-blown invasion of America, Mr. Trump had to lose the 2020 presidential election. But with a roaring economy, that was unlikely.

So, it is not surprisingly that the 2020 presidential election turned out to be the shadiest in U.S. history. With massive evidence of voter fraud only in "swing states," unsurprisingly, Mr. Obama's FBI found nothing amiss. That would be the same FBI that illegally surveilled Trump's 2016 campaign. It took citizen reporters to uncover the depth of fraud that took place, which appeared to be more than enough to throw the election to Mr. Biden. It appears that the powers to be wanted Mr. Biden in power.

Still concerned that President Trump could return to office in 2024, in 2022 Mr. Biden appointed another Special Counsel to investigate him after an unprecedented raid by the FBI at his home. Mysteriously, after the raid, disturbing photos surfaced that showed classified documents carelessly strewn across the floor. Later, it would be revealed that the FBI staged it. Essentially, it was FBI propaganda. No such documents had been found in that condition. Instead, they were arranged for a photo op. And naturally, after the raid, the Special Counsel found what he claimed were violations of law that required Trump to be criminally charged. Ironically, the exact same kind of documents were discovered in Mr. Biden's possession while Vice President. But the DOJ saw no crime.

Considering the litany of corrupt practices that have been taking place, there are questions to ponder. Such as would those engaged in allowing an invasion of America hesitate for one moment to steal a presidential election. Would they hesitate to unleash a virus across the world to destroy President Trump's chances of getting reelected? Would they be willing to turn the FBI and DOJ into third-world law enforcement agencies to go after their main enemy? Would they attempt an assassination against Mr. Trump using a 20-year-old? One who was granted access to a sniper's nest only 130 yards from where the former president was speaking. A twenty-year-old who had several overseas encrypted accounts. And after the shooting, whose home was cleaned of fingerprints as though a professional crew swept it. A twenty-year-old in which cell phone tracking ping data revealed a phone that visited the shooters home and work several times, then went back to an area in Washington, D.C., near both FBI and Secret Service buildings. It was also reported that some entity took a very large short position on Truth Social, Trump's social media company that is traded on the stock exchange. Coincidentally, this unusually large, highly risky bet was placed only days before the attempted assassination. Had President Trump been killed the value of the stock would have plunged, reaping a huge payoff to any short positions. How did this entity know to suddenly do that only days before the assassination attempt? Obviously, the FBI "investigation" into the assassination attempt will whitewash all signs of a conspiracy. Behind it all can be only one man. The man who corrupted the FBI and DOJ.

Adding to the litany of discoveries is that Mr. Biden was not mentally fit to be president. Raising serious questions as to who has been running the nation. When that question is asked, most people say Mr. Obama. It was Mr. Obama who swung the support of Congressman James Clyburn of South Carolina, which kept alive Mr. Biden's 2020 presidential hopes after he had already lost the first two contests, and his campaign was on the ropes. Then suddenly, after winning only one primary, all other Democratic contenders dropped out of the presidential race even before Super Tuesday. A first in the history of primaries. Only Mr. Obama could pull off something like that. Those who think Mr. Obama has been running the country during Mr. Biden's term may be on to something. Mr. Biden certainly could not. Which may explain why Mr. Obama is the only former U.S. president who stayed in Washington, D.C., after he left office. Because he never really left the office. All pointing to it really being Mr. Obama who has kept the border wide open.

There is something strange about how Mr. Obama rose to the presidency that few people know about. His rise was unlike any other in American history. The following is a rendition of his rise, step by step all the way to the presidency. Then you, the reader, decide if he was just incredibly lucky or if there was a super powerful force guiding him all the way to the White House. Wherein he then instituted not only the most anti-Christian actions in American history but began corrupting federal law enforcement agencies with political activists. And if he has been the real power behind Mr. Biden, a man that now we can understand has been only a puppet, then the army that has entered America is Barack's Army.

THE RISE OF BARACK OBAMA

Barack Obama was the most unlikely type to become President of the United States. And it had nothing to do with his race. His "pastor" was Jeremiah Wright. A man whose recorded sermons included virulent anti-Americanism.[1] An advisor to him was Ms. Anita Dunn. An admirer of the late Chinese leader Mao Zedong, whose reign included the mass killings of millions.[2] Also included in this police lineup were William Ayres and his wife, Bernadine Dorn. Former Weather Underground terrorists.[3]

THE ILLINOIS STATE SENATE "RACE"

The first office Mr. Obama ran for in his rise to the presidency was that of state senator in 1996. In order to qualify as a candidate for the Illinois State Senate, there is a requirement that the candidate acquire the signatures of at least 750 voters within the district favoring their candidacy. However, all the candidates played it safe by gathering many more signatures than necessary. Like Alice Palmer, the popular incumbent senator running for re-election. She gathered 1,580 signatures.[4]

However, despite the massive overkill of signatures submitted by each candidate, including the incumbent, the Chicago Board of Elections threw out enough signatures on each to the point where none qualified to have their names placed on the ballot. Including the incumbent! The only candidate whose signatures were not challenged. Mr. Barack Obama. Thus started his rise.[5]

THE U.S. SENATE

In 2004 state senator Obama was ready to take the next step. Or, more accurately, the hidden force behind him was ready to elevate him to the next political position. The United States Senate. As a coveted high political office, there were also others seeking it. Enormously powerful political leaders. One was a very well-known and well-funded Democrat named Blair Hull, who easily became the party's main candidate. As such, the vast majority of Democratic politicians in Illinois rallied behind the Hull campaign. On the Republican side, there was another well-funded and well-known candidate. His name was Jack Ryan.[6]

A s the election cycle progressed Mr. Obama was hardly register-ing in the pools. However, then something strange began unfolding. Suddenly and relentlessly, the Chicago Tribune began hammering on the divorce records of both Hull and Ryan. Their sudden interest in divorce a surprise. One "scandal" after another relating to their divorces was unleashed. Finally, the unrelenting assault against the character of both men had its desired effect. Hull and Ryan discon-tinued their campaigns and withdrew their candidacies. Making State Senator Barack Obama the inevitable new U.S. Senator for the State of Illinois.[7, 8]

But the hidden force behind him was ready to immediately elevate him to an even higher level. An introduction to the nation through the 2004 Democratic Presidential Convention. While he was still only a state senator! Something never before done.

THE 2004 DEMOCRATIC CONVENTION

The 2004 Democratic Convention took a new approach. Granting the keynote address to the state senator from Illinois, Mr. Barack Obama. Whose fame was that he was running for the U.S. Senate. An unheard-of elevation of a complete unknown.[9,10] What influ-ence! Upon delivering the keynote address, all major media outlets immediately began reading from the same playbook. Creating the narrative that Obama's speech was one of the greatest keynote addresses' ever given. And with all singing from the same page, they immediately began speaking of Obama as a 2008 presidential candidate.

THE 2008 PRESIDENTIAL CAMPAIGN

As a candidate for the Democratic nomination for president, Mr. Obama ran a campaign centered on "fundamentally transforming America." A strange statement coming from a virtual unknown. And one that created questions in the minds of voters. His opponent in the race was the long-time U.S. Senator John McCain, once a prisoner of war.

With McCain a known quantity and Obama telling the nation he wished to "fundamentally transform" it, polling naturally showed the newcomer several points behind his Republican opponent with just six weeks remaining. Despite major pushes by the mainstream media to elevate him and the suppression of information critical of him. His amazing streak of "good luck" had finally come to an end. Then the hidden kingdom flexed its muscles.

A FINANCIAL COLLAPSE TO THE RESCUE

Six weeks before election day, something happened that had not occurred since the 1930s. Financial institutions that were the bedrock of the American banking system began to collapse in rapid succession. With the Republican Bush Administration taking the brunt of the blame. And what precipitated the sudden collapse was unusual.

The Bush Administration had been bailing out multiple financial institutions over the previous year to keep the nation's financial system from cascading into a complete meltdown. And thus far, throughout 2008, the administration had very adroitly and successfully succeeded in preventing the worst from happening through bailouts.[11]

But with only six weeks remaining in a presidential election, the Bush Administration suddenly refused to bail out a key institution. It was the highly interconnected investment banking giant Lehman Brothers. The collapse of which was guaranteed to cause financial contagion. The decision not to help Lehman Brothers is credited to Treasury Secretary Hank Paulson. As a former CEO of Goldman Sachs, one of the most connected financial institutions in the world. Paulson single-handedly enabled this collapse with his decision to suddenly reverse policy.[12] It was as though Mr. Paulson wanted to elect the unknown senator from Illinois to the presidency. And that is exactly what happened.

THE HIDDEN KINGDOM

Within various circles there is much talk about an international entity operating behind the scenes that exercises massive power over governments across the world. The most common name for it is the New World Order. Whatever name it is called by it has become clear that some global force has been guiding nations in a very dark direction. Unfortunately, it has become clear in recent years that the United States is one of those nations. It is apparent from the record of how Mr. Obama rose to the presidency that there was a powerful force behind him. One able to void the candidacies of an incumbent state senator along with others vying for public office. Demonstrating a powerful corrupt influence on a local level. Then, on a statewide level, that same force was able to drive two powerful Illinois politicians out of a U.S. Senate race. Leaving that high and coveted political office, Mr. Obama's for the taking. It was so influential that the highly desired role of keynote speaker at the 2004 Democratic National Convention was granted to the then state senator. Another first. When Mr. Obama was in the presidential race coincidentally the rug got pulled out from the financial system with just weeks before the election. With the obvious result being that voters would blame the Republican Party. Thus, helping Mr. Obama overcome his Republican opponent and win the election.

It might be said that Mr. Obama has been a 12-year president considering the influence he had over the Biden Administration. Clearly, one of his main goals was a wide-open border. Is it a coincidence that as if on que upon taking power, Mr. Biden began opening the border as wide as possible? With a host of executive orders directing government agencies to actively invite foreigners into the country with offers of welfare. Is it a coincidence that upon Mr. Biden/Obama taking power that it was in early 2021 the makeup of people crossing the border into America began to change. With tens of thousands of military age single men from hostile regions and countries coming across. A coincidence? Or part of Mr. Obama's plan?

Obviously, to remain in control of the White House Mr. Obama must have a loyal Democrat as president. Loyal to him that is. But that is where Mr. Biden began presenting a problem. Within the upper circles of the Democratic Party Mr. Biden's mental impairments were well known. This is why he was kept almost invisible to the public throughout his term. He was incapable of speaking without making people wonder about his mental facilities. But it is very hard to tell a sitting president he cannot run for reelection. So, a plan was hatched. That plan was to expose his problem as early in the election year as possible to have time to drive him out of the race. Craftily, instead of having the traditional presidential debates start in September after both parties nominated their candidates, the Biden team sought a much earlier debate. The first held in May. Three months early!

Knowing he would experience a complete collapse before the nation, the hope was that he would voluntarily depart the race realizing his chance of winning just evaporated. However, even though his debate performance was terrible, it was reported that Mr. Biden was refusing to give way to the forces that were demanding he step down from running. After Mr. Trump took a sizable lead in the polls after the debate, it was then that two historical events unfolded in rapid succession.

1ST: AN ASSASSINATION ATTEMPT

There was an assassination attempt against President Trump. The timing of which was only a few days before the Republican Convention. That attempt failed only by the grace of God. Associated with the attempt is an array of information pointing to a conspiracy. In fact, it was set up so well that those behind the effort must have been amazed that it failed. The shooter was granted access to within 130 yards of President Trump. It was a simple shot. But as the bullet was traveling in the air Trump was in the process of moving his head resulting in it grazing his right ear instead of exploding the back of his head. Had the attempt succeeded then the Republican Party would be without a leader to nominate only a few days before the convention. The result would chaos and a deeply split party with little chance of winning. After the failed attempt the next big thing happened only a week later.

2ND: A COUP

Celebrated reporter Seymour Hersch, who broke the My Lai massacre story during the Vietnam war, and later the story that the Biden Administration was behind the attack on the Russian gas pipeline in the North Sea, also got the inside scoop on Mr. Biden's pulling out of the presidential race. According to Hersch it was a coup.

Sources in the White House told Hersch that Mr. Obama was the impetus behind pushing Mr. Biden out. According to Hersch, "I went over [reports] this week with a senior official in Washington who helped me fashion an account of a White House in complete disarray." According to his source, Mr. Obama called Mr. Biden and told him that he had the approval of Vice President Harris, Nancy Pelosi, Chuck Schumer, and Hakeem Jeffries to invoke the 25 Amendment removing him from office unless he withdrew from the presidential race. But something else his source told him is of special interest as it relates to the invasion of America.

The source told Hersch that Obama would not immediately endorse Harris but would wait a few days. Although he made it clear that she would "get the nod." Further saying that Obama "had an agenda and he wanted to see it through to the end, and he wanted to have control over who would be elected." In other words, Mr. Obama wants to complete the process of fundamentally changing America. And the main way of doing that is to keep the invasion of America going.

Interestingly, Mr. Obama at the beginning of his presidency called for a "civilian national security force." Something unheard of in American history. At a speech in Colorado, Mr. Obama called for expanding the nation's foreign service to include a domestic force. "We've got to have a civilian national security force that's just as powerful, just as strong, just as well funded." One congressman in response to the legislation introduced to establish this force called it "Obama's Gestapo-like force. It was rejected.[13]

With the passage of time and the litany of dictatorial actions directed against the enemies of Mr. Obama and his party, it is now clear how such a federal "national security force" would have been used. All of which raises the question if the rejection of that force ultimately resulted in a change of plans. That being the importation of an army through the southern border.

10

STEPS TO BE TAKEN

That there is a war coming to American soil is almost certain. Armies from China, Africa, and the Middle East have flooded across the southern border coinciding with Mr. Biden taking power. Which can be no coincidence that Mr. Obama has been the real power behind the throne. His openly stated goal was to fundamentally change America. Although he is well on his way to doing so, he apparently needed a large foreign army to enter the United States to complete the process. Considering what has taken place since 2021, it is critically important that every loyal American begin taking certain steps to protect their family and to save America for future generations. The first step is to appreciate certain things about the armies that have entered.

Many come from areas of the world where utter brutality in war is the norm. Wonton killing of men, women and children is part of that norm. As is rape. And considering the hatred most likely have for America, they will exercise unrestrained brutality. A good example of how Americans will be treated was demonstrated when Israel suffered an invasion by Hamas in 2023 from the Gaza region. Approximately 3000 Hamas militants slaughtered over 1400 Israelis. They also systematically raped hundreds of hostages taken in the raid. Since many of the Middle Easterners who have invaded have seen America engaged in multiple wars in their region, their resulting hatred for this country will result in their engaging in actions like what Hamas did to the Israelis. Because many of the Middle East invaders have seen much death and destruction in their own lands, they will look forward to bringing it to America whom they hold responsible.

For the Chinese invaders they believe that their nation has the right to be the hegemon over the world. That means to be the dominant world power. This is like the notion of manifest destiny that guided Americans in the 1800s to conquer the North American continent from the Atlantic to the Pacific. Such beliefs are a powerful driving force behind any military. America standing firm in support of Taiwan is seen in China as a great affront against their nation. Providing them with a sense of needing to settle a score. Bringing America into their sights as an enemy. These invaders will be brutal as well.

For those elements that are an organized army, like the Chinese, they will have battle plan which almost certainly involves taking out key infrastructure sites across the US. Shutting down communications, electricity, sewage, transportation, food supplies and a host of other services. And with a hidden army possibly in the hundreds of thousands, they have the means to bring America to her knees.

They will attack power stations as well as transformer stations. The shutdown of power could last for many months, making it critical to have enough supplies to make it through the rough early part. Which means an alternative power source. As well as several months of food, water, medicine and other supplies forming an important part of life.

It is also necessary to be well armed for personal protection. Including body armor and night vision and lots of ammo. If your neighborhood is targeted, you will literally be defending your family and home. There will also be a natural gathering together of locals in common defense. Join then but make certain whoever is leading the defense of your neighborhood has military experience.

There is another consideration, and it relates to the deceptive nature of those in power who are responsible for allowing the army within America. It is likely when the attack comes that if the government is run by Democrats, they will deceive the public about what is really happening. One possibility is claiming "white supremacist" are attacking causing confusion. It will take a period before those deceived will understand what is really happening.

What will determine how long and bloody the coming war will be will largely depend on what party is in the White House. If it is in the hands of the Democratic Party, then it should be expected that powerful elements will assist the invaders. This is because of the fact that they actively enabled their army entry into the country. Making Vidkum Quisling look like a patriot in comparison. Of course, it should be expected that they will use their control over "legacy media" to spread disinformation. They may even attempt to take guns away claiming this will solve the problem. DO NOT GIVE UP YOUR GUNS NO MATTER WHAT. They may also begin placing Americans resisting the invaders in camps. DO NOT GO NO MATTER WHAT. A Democratic Administration in power at the time the army attacks will result in a very long and bloody war.

If Republicans are in the White House the response will be radically different. The enemy army are not fools. So, there will likely be an attempt to take out the president by use of any means at their disposal. And due to the line of succession, if a Democrat is leading the House of Representatives, being second in line to the presidency, this will place both a Republican President and Vice President in harm's way when the foreign armies launch their attack. Because success against both would result in the Democrat being elevated into the White House.

This is because the invaders know that if America has a president with the will to fight it represents a major asset in time of war. This author believes small nukes will be used in the opening battle per the epilogue following this chapter. It should also be expected that even if a Republican Administration is in power that treasonous elements still in key positions will do all they can to thwart the response of the government against the invaders. Including a strong disinformation campaign carried out by all Democratic media outlets.

Perhaps the most significant step to confront what is coming is one that a community can take. And that is for local police departments to recruit a strong volunteer civilian auxiliary force to augment their professional policy force. Under the command of the local police department, this volunteer citizen force would be able to supply massive additional resources in the event their town or area is one targeted by a large contingent of enemy forces. Considering the potential size of the foreign army that has entered, it is quite possible that concentrated attacks will overwhelm local police. How would your town handle a force of 500 or even 1,000 vicious armed fighters attacking? In towns with a police force of under 500 most law enforcement officers will lose their lives leaving a disorganized resistance to carry on the fight. And since attacks in such numbers will be happening in many locations at one time, there may be no help coming from outside to save the lives of countless citizens. But a police force augmented with a citizen auxiliary force of 500 volunteers under their command, the attackers in that scenario will face utter destruction. A basic requirement of such a volunteer force will be a method of communication to each volunteer that cannot be taken down with the grid.

It is critically important that all auxiliary forces be under the command of local police departments. Because they are not only best equipped to handle local attacks, but it also eliminates the ability of treasonous elements in the federal government from taking command over them as they can with state National Guard units. If the local police department cannot be convinced of the threat and has no desire to augment their force with such an auxiliary force, then gun clubs should be started. Allowing for the common defense of neighborhoods and key local infrastructure.

Most importantly in preparing for what is coming is placing faith in Jesus Christ as Lord and Savior. It was such faith that saw the Revolutionary War heroes through the darkest days of that war. Scripture tells us that no greater love has a man than to lay down his life for another. And the willingness to stand and fight against these foreign armies when they attack should be viewed in the same light. Because wherever they go will follow death and destruction to countless innocent people.

So, stand in faith and stand firm!

EPILOGUE:
A PROPHETIC DREAM

As Americans watch the flood of dangerous individuals cross the southern border, the demographics of which dramatically changed only after Mr. Biden took power, a literal enemy army has been forming within America. The ten former FBI leaders estimate the size of these armies is in the league of several military divisions. But it could easily be even larger. This nightmare scenario has befallen America only with the beginning of the strange Biden Administration. The first in history where it is clear the president is someone else's puppet. Under a puppet master clearly with malice toward America and Christianity.

What is of the greatest significance is that the prophetic words of Isaiah now are unfolding in terrible detail. With large numbers of those "from a far country" entering America with the help of United Nations non-government organizations who then distribute them across the country. These non-government organizations are at the heart and soul of the United Nations. Which itself is a tool of the fabled New World Order. The size of the foreign military within the United States could number as many as a few hundreds of thousands. Destined to bring a level of death and destruction to American soil that will dwarf losses from even the Civil War. Presenting America with the greatest threat in her history.

With the gathering of these armies, Isaiah's prophecy is setting up as foretold. Interestingly, so is that of the vision that George Washington experienced while suffering the winter of 1777-78 at Valley Forge. If Washington did, in fact, experience the vision as relayed by Mr. Sherman, then it is unfolding along the lines indicated back in 1880, when the earliest article relaying it can be found.

A Prophetic Dream

This author feels the need to relay a prophetic dream I experienced back in 2009. The reason why is that events in recent years are unfolding in such a way that I feel I must now share it. Let me add that I certainly understand the hearing of the dreams and visions of men requires great discernment. I typically never pay much mind to such things. However, I personally cannot deny the previous prophetic dreams I received from the Lord since they unfolded as given. Nor can I deny the uniqueness of such dreams and the inability to forget them. Unlike natural dreams, those from the Lord remain etched in the recipient's memory. And current events are now making sense out of parts of that dream that previously were not clear.

On the evening of January 23, 2009, three days after the inauguration of Barack Obama to the presidency, the Lord gave me a prophetic dream. It was of the same unique nature as prior dreams from him. Those previous dreams foretold events that were either heading my way or toward a family member. Each was of the same unique nature, and each unfolded as foretold. As mentioned earlier, dreams from the Lord are remembered long after they are given, unlike natural dreams. From a personal standpoint, I find relaying the following prophetic dream very difficult. But I do not have any choice.

The Lord showed me two small planes flying through Central Florida toward the Atlantic coast. Both stayed just inland. One plane, which I will call the first, veered south along the coast, and the second took a more northerly course toward Cape Canaveral. I was not shown how far south the first plane went. Only that it went south. Shockingly, I was shown a fireball from the detonation of a nuclear weapon from the first plane. Then I was shown another fireball detonation from the second plane, which exploded just south of the Cape.

Upon waking, I was stunned by what I saw. Having experienced several other prophetic dreams from the Lord, I immediately knew this one was from Him as well. That day I mentioned it to some friends and family members. Since I had not relayed the prior dreams to them, the impact was marginal. In relaying the dream, I found that most people inquired as to when it would happen. Something I did not know at that time. The other question was why the east coast of Florida. Why not New York or Washington, D.C.? That too I did not understand. At that time all I knew was that the dream was from the Lord since it possessed the same qualities as the others. And that it was clearly showing nuclear detonations that would take place on the east coast of Florida sometime in the future.

Not having any idea as to when this would happen caused me to begin praying every evening for the knowledge of when it would take place. After about two months of praying for that knowledge, the Lord generously answered that prayer. And He did so in an unusual way.

It was a Friday evening in March 2009, and once again before retiring, I asked for knowledge of when the horrific event would take place. As I awoke the next morning, I stayed in bed for a while thinking about all the things I had to do that day. Suddenly, I began experiencing a sense of intense goodness gathering in the bedroom. Being a unique experience, I wondered what was happening. The goodness finally reached a crescendo after about 30 seconds. Whereupon I heard in my heart, "When they say Peace." Thereafter, the goodness began to dissipate until everything was back to normal again.

Sitting up in bed, I began wondering what had just happened. Because it was an experience that I had never had, there was no prior reference to go back to. But soon it began to dawn on me that the word I received was in response to my prayers. I also realized it came straight from scripture. In 1 Thessalonians 5:1-3 we are told, "When they say, 'Peace and safety!' then sudden destruction comes upon them, as labor pains upon a woman." Prophetic birth pangs. The sudden beginning of the day of the Lord. The end times.

We know from Jesus' words in the Olivet Discourse that at the beginning of the day of the Lord (end times), nations will suddenly "rise" to war against one another. We know from His prophet Isaiah that some of the attacks will be directed against nations from within. With the invasion at the southern border allowing multiple enemy military divisions within, America will certainly be one of those struck from within. What the Lord showed me is that at the launch of the attack on America, two nuclear weapons will be detonated. What He showed me in the prophetic dream is in line with the sudden destruction associated with the start of the day of the Lord. It simply describes a particular detail of a specific attack. An attack that will only be a small part of a much greater war engulfing the entire world.

Understanding the dream in context with prophetic scripture was a gift from the Lord. But it still left unanswered the question as to why the east coast of Florida would be targeted. But events in recent years are beginning to bring clarity to that question as well. And the answer must be President Trump and his home in Mar-a-Lago, Florida. It is an effort to kill him to prevent America from having a true leader when the enemy army attacks. I can think of no other reason.

DANIEL'S PROPHECY

The Lord sees the beginning from the end, and all His prophecies will eventually come to pass. Although Isaiah's prophecy indicates America will face the greatest challenge in her history, the perspective I will hold on to as tightly as possible is that of Daniel's. The perspective on Daniel's lion, leopard, and bear prophecy presented in this book offers hope for America. In a sense, so does Isaiah's, because eventually the foreign forces gathering inside America will be driven out. And America will be set free.

REFERENCES

Chapter Two References

1. Gordon Chang, Fox News 'Mornings with Maria,'
2. Invaded: The Intentional Destruction of the American Immigration System, John Carrell, June 2023
3. Ibid.
4. Ibid.
5. Ibid.
6. Times of India, "Donald Trump: Chinese Migrants Forming an Army in US," May 2023
7. Ibid.
8. Documentary, "Destiny of America," Jimmy Deyoung
9. Ibid.

Chapter Three

1. Jennifer-Leigh Oprihory, "People Tried to Breach Air National Guard Bases at Least 13 Times This Year," *Air & Space Forces Magazine*
2. Gordon Lubold, Warren Strobel, Aruna Viswanatha, "Chinese Gate-Crashers at U.S. Bases Spark Espionage Concerns," The wWall Street Journal

3. Darlene McCormick Sanchez, "Chinese May Be Probing American Military Through Base Breaches, Lawmaker Says," The Epoch Times

4. Darlene McCormick Sanchez, "Chinese May Be Probing American Military Through Base Breaches, Lawmaker Says," The Epoch Times

5. Head of Fleet Command Says Foreign Nationals Trying to Breach Bases Weekly, Defense Community News

6. Kari Jacobson, "Two Illegal Aliens Attempt to Breach U.S. Military Base, Dangerous Trend Continues Under Biden", Federation for American Immigration Reform

7. Kari Jacobson, "Two Illegal Aliens Attempt to Breach U.S. Military Base, Dangerous Trend Continues Under Biden", Federation for American Immigration Reform

8. Kari Jacobson, "Two Illegal Aliens Attempt to Breach U.S. Military Base, Dangerous Trend Continues Under Biden", Federation for American Immigration Reform

9. Kari Jacobson, "Two Illegal Aliens Attempt to Breach U.S. Military Base, Dangerous Trend Continues Under Biden", Federation for American Immigration Reform

10. The Epoch Times, Darlene Sanchez, "US Increases Scrutiny of Chinese Land Buys Near Military Bases," July 2024

11. Zero Hedge, August 5, 2024, "Two Chinese Nationals in U.S. Illegally Stopped With $250,000 In Gold Bars on Them in Texas."

Chapter Nine

1. The Obama Files, http://the obamafile.com/_associates/obamaas-sociates.htm

2. The Obama Files, http://the obamafile.com/_associates/obamaas-sociates.htm

3. The Obama Files, http://the obamafile.com/_associates/obamaas-sociates.htm

4. Jay Stone, "Obama Strategy to Win at All Costs Violated his Challengers' Civil Rights," http://stoneformayor.com/obama s-strategy-to-win-at-all-costs-violated-his-challengers-civil-rights/

5. Ibid

6. Fox News, Ryan Drops Out of Ill. Senate Race," 06/25/2004, http://www.foxnews.com/story/0,2933,123716,00.html

7. Dennis W., Free republic, "David Axelrod---Gets Obama's opponent's sealed divorce records opened up," 9/6/2008, http://www.freerepublic.com/focus/news/2075850/posts

8. Ibid

9. Steve Kornacki, New York Observer, "A Brief History of Democratic Convention Keynotes," http://observer.com/2008/08/a-brief-history-of-democratic-convention-keynoters/

10. Ibid

11. Nick Mathiason, The Guardian, "Three weeks that changed the world," http://www.guardian.co.uk/business/2008/dec/28/markets-credit-crunch-banking-2008

12. Ibid

13. NBC News, "Congressman: Obama wants a Gestapo-Like force," https://www.nbcnews.com/id/wbna27655039

www.ingramcontent.com/pod-product-compliance
Lightning Source LLC
Chambersburg PA
CBHW052053270326
41931CB00012B/2740